D0983979

Financial Regulation and Compliance

The Wiley Finance series contains books written specifically for finance and investment professionals as well as sophisticated individual investors and their financial advisors. Book topics range from portfolio management to e-commerce, risk management, financial engineering, valuation and financial instrument analysis, as well as much more. For a list of available titles, visit our Web site at www.WileyFinance.com.

Founded in 1807, John Wiley & Sons is the oldest independent publishing company in the United States. With offices in North America, Europe, Australia and Asia, Wiley is globally committed to developing and marketing print and electronic products and services for our customers' professional and personal knowledge and understanding.

Financial Regulation and Compliance

How to Manage Competing and Overlapping Regulatory Oversight

H. DAVID KOTZ

WILEY

Published by John Wiley & Sons, Inc., Hoboken, New Jersey.

For general information about our other products and services, please contact our Customer Care Department within the United States at (800) 762-2974, outside the United States at (317) 572-3993 or fax (317) 572-4002.

Wiley publishes in a variety of print and electronic formats and by print-on-demand. Some material included with standard print versions of this book may not be included in e-books or in print-on-demand. If this book refers to media such as a CD or DVD that is not included in the version you purchased, you may download this material at http://booksupport.wiley.com. For more information about Wiley products, visit www.wiley.com

Library of Congress Cataloging-in-Publication Data

Kotz, H. David, author.
 Financial regulation and compliance : how to manage competing and overlapping regulatory oversight / H. David Kotz.
     pages cm. – (The wiley finance series)
   Includes index.
   ISBN 978-1-118-97221-2 (hardback)
 1. Financial institutions–Law and legislation–United States. I. Title.
   KF974.K68 2015
   346.73'08–dc23   2015017704

ISBN 978-1-118-97221-2 (hbk)
ISBN 978-1-118-97223-6 (ebk)
ISBN 978-1-118-97222-9 (ebk)
ISBN 978-1-118-97224-3 (ebk)

Cover Design: Wiley
Cover Images: Top image ©iStock.com/scyther5; Bottom image ©iStock.com/jwohlfeil

Printed in the United States of America

10 9 8 7 6 5 4 3 2 1

To my wife, Debbie, and my three children, Shira, Joshua and Ruven, who inspire and support me on a daily basis, and who mean everything to me.

Contents

Foreword

Few topics in finance are more confusing to outsiders than regulation. There are many among us who understand financial valuation and even the technical intricacies of the esoteric contingent claims analysis, copula functions, and risk mapping algorithms. But the supervision and regulation of banks, much less securities firms, tend to make the eyes of most financial analysts glaze over.

Yet the compliance function is one of the most important, and valuable, functions in any financial institution. Compliance is more than just records retention. As recent crisis-era litigation has shown, managing compliance properly can help reduce vast legal costs later. While we may not want to admit it, compliance creates value.

The problem is that not many people – whether they be financial practitioners, policymakers, or sometimes even compliance professionals – really understand compliance. Part of the problem is the unique path dependence that has created a fractured supervisory structure with some delineations by institution and some by function, creating considerable regulatory overlap. Even understanding who is responsible for what, in any real sense, after accounting for "primary" supervisory responsibility, can be massively confusing.

This became apparent to me when I began to advise staff at the European Union (EU) Parliament on their own reforms to financial regulation. At the time the U.S. was (and is still) urging them to just adopt U.S. institutional features, which EU staff did not understand. Thereupon, we embarked on an almost two-year project to educate the staff in this massively tangled and – to the uninitiated – thoroughly confusing framework for U.S. financial supervision.

The problem became even worse when we ran into the subject of administrative law – that is, regulation – and also its enforcement, venues for defense, and appeal. While I was able to treat the subjects in just a few areas (primarily banking) with a wide variety of existing resources, the present manuscript pulls together far more material in a single volume than ever before published on the subject.

Moreover, this book's treatment of securities regulation pushes into a much newer area of financial supervision, covering the securities sector. Historically, only banks were supervised – that is, subjected to examinations that required producing confidential records to supervisory personnel with the threat of sanctions. But in recent years, the SEC's examination function has grown significantly, and if some policymakers have their way, it will continue to grow.

In conjunction with such growth, some of the more troubling aspects of bank regulation seem to be spilling over into securities regulation. In the 2015 examination priorities of the Office of Compliance Inspections and Examinations (OCIE), the SEC is putting more emphasis on "using data analytics to identify signals of potential illegal activity." The idea is that trading or payment patterns can indicate firms or brokers that are "potentially engaged in fraudulent and/or other potential illegal activity." Thus, analytical exercises are used to determine who might run afoul of anti-money laundering or other related restrictions.

The idea is generally good, but the implementation in the banking world has been fraught with controversy. The U.S. Treasury has pushed bank regulators to undertake similar programs related to Operation Choke Point in recent years. In addition, recently, the FDIC has sought to disassociate itself from the approach after some banks and companies were tremendously hurt by investigations that turned out to be for naught. The point is that while certain patterns of business behavior might be associated with criminal activity (like high chargeback rates on credit cards in the retail sector), there is little to distinguish those from legitimate activity in business that merely operates on almost identical principles. That is why fraud works.

The author of this book is the former Inspector General of the SEC and has been fortunate to see firsthand how regulations are supposed to work, and how they are often perceived by the regulated community. I have been an admirer of his work at the SEC for quite some time, as he was able to conduct meaningful oversight of a very important financial regulator during a very significant time period in our nation's financial history. In this book, he draws on his own vast experience to provide cogent hands-on advice to compliance professionals in a myriad of important areas. He also brings together a very unique collection of expertise from many individuals, including several former senior-level governmental officials which only add to the comprehensiveness and value of this book. It is a must-read for compliance professionals in the financial arena, and, as supervisory principles are applied in financial market regulation, the present manuscript will be all the more important to manage the new regulatory and administrative law burdens that will be imposed on the industry.

Joseph R. Mason, the Hermann Moyse, Jr./ Louisiana Bankers Association Endowed Chair of Banking and Professor of Finance at Louisiana State University and Senior Fellow at the Wharton School.

Preface

During the week of March 10, 2008, I was in the first few months of my new position as Inspector General of the Securities and Exchange Commission ("SEC"). I had come over to the SEC after serving as Inspector General of the Peace Corps. At the Peace Corps, I dealt with many very significant issues, some involving life and death, as I tried to put into place procedures for ensuring Peace Corps Volunteer safety and security. Much of my time was spent working with foreign governments to assist in the prosecution of individuals who committed heinous crimes against Peace Corps Volunteers, such as assault, rape, and even murder. I found my job very rewarding and many of the protections we put into place for Volunteers remain in existence today. The Peace Corps position was, however, generally low profile, and while I testified before Congress on one or two occasions during my tenure as Inspector General of the Peace Corps, for the most part, we were able to operate out of the public eye. I recall when I interviewed for the SEC position that former Chairman Christopher Cox told me, at the end of my interview, words to the effect of "one thing you will realize if you work here, this is not going to be like working at the Peace Corps." Chairman Cox certainly turned out to be right about that statement.

I was the second ever Inspector General in the SEC's history. The previous Inspector General had been in his position for approximately 18 years, and had recently retired among some rumblings from Capitol Hill that his office could have been more aggressive in certain investigations. Shortly after I arrived at the SEC at the very end of 2007, I received a letter from Senator Charles E. Grassley (R-Iowa), who was then the Ranking Member of the United States

Senate Committee on Finance, referencing the previous Inspector General's tenure and pointing out that he expected my office to engage in aggressive oversight. I understood that I was being watched carefully and expectations were high regarding my tenure as Inspector General.

I very clearly recall the extreme concern at the SEC during the week of March 10, 2008, when word spread about liquidity problems at Bear Stearns. There was also, of course, a flurry of activity surrounding the March 16, 2008 Bear Stearns' sale to JP Morgan with financing support from the Federal Reserve Bank of New York ("FRBNY"). Little did I realize at that time how significant these events would be not only in my own life, but with respect to its role in the eventual global financial crisis.

On April 2, 2008, my office received another letter from Ranking Member Grassley, requesting that my office analyze the SEC's oversight of firms under its Consolidated Supervised Entity ("CSE") program and broker-dealers subject to the SEC's Risk Assessment Program. The letter requested a review of the SEC's oversight of the investment banks that it supervised, with a special emphasis on Bear Stearns. The letter requested that we analyze the adequacy of the SEC's monitoring of Bear Stearns, and that we make recommendations to improve the SEC programs.

The CSE program was a voluntary program created by the SEC in 2004, to allow the SEC to supervise certain broker-dealer holding companies on a consolidated basis. These entities included Bear Stearns, Lehman Brothers, Goldman Sachs, Morgan Stanley, Merrill Lynch, Citigroup Inc., and JP Morgan. The CSE program was designed to allow the SEC to monitor for financial or operational weakness in a CSE holding company or its unregulated affiliates that might place regulated broker-dealers and other regulated entities at risk. The CSE program's mission was, in pertinent part as follows:

> *The regime is intended to allow the Commission to monitor for, and act quickly in response to, financial or operational weakness in a CSE holding company or its unregulated affiliates that might place regulated entities, including*

US and foreign-registered banks and . . . broker-dealers, or
the broader financial system at risk. *(emphasis added.)*[1]

I understood at that point in time how important it was for there
to be a thorough and comprehensive assessment of the circumstances
that led to Bear Stearns' collapse and the effectiveness of the CSE
program, and I was very aware that my office was being given
an opportunity to demonstrate that we could engage in aggressive
oversight of the SEC and its programs. Accordingly, I decided that
I would not "pull any punches" with respect to this assessment
and audit, and determined that one of my initial conclusions in my
assessment would be that "it is undisputable that the CSE program
failed to carry out its mission in its oversight of Bear Stearns because
under the Commission and the CSE program's watch, Bear Stearns
suffered significant financial weaknesses and the FRBNY needed to
intervene during the week of March 10, 2008, to prevent significant
harm to the broader financial system."[2]

In the audit, we also found numerous specific concerns with
the SEC's oversight of the CSE program, including the fact that,
although the SEC was aware, prior to Bear Stearns becoming a
CSE firm, that Bear Stearns' concentration of mortgage securities
had been increasing for several years and was beyond its internal
limits, and that a portion of Bear Stearns' mortgage securities (e.g.,
adjustable rate mortgages) represented a significant concentration
of market risk, the SEC did not make any efforts to limit Bear
Stearns' mortgage securities concentration. We also did not "pull
any punches" with respect to Bear Stearns, as we concluded that
there was evidence of significant shortcomings in the area of risk
management at Bear Stearns, including a proximity of Bear Stearns'
risk managers to traders suggesting a lack of independence.

There was a strong reaction within the SEC as a result of our findings, and concerns were expressed about the impact of the report on

---

[1] See *SEC's Oversight of Bear Stearns and Related Entities: The Consolidated Supervised Entity Program*, SEC Office of Inspector General, Report No. 446-A, September 25, 2008, at http://www.sec.gov/about/oig/audit/2008/446-a.pdf.
[2] Ibid. at p. viii.

the SEC's reputation and credibility, which could negatively affect its ability to engage in regulatory oversight. There were even comments made that a weakened SEC as a result of my office's report would make it more difficult for the government to manage what was increasingly being viewed as the beginning of a serious financial crisis, and suggestions about whether the entire report should be publicly disclosed. Notwithstanding these concerns, I decided that it was more important for Congress and the public to understand what had occurred with respect to Bear Stearns' collapse and the SEC's oversight, and I declined to substantially edit the report and released it with minimal redactions.

Congressional officials appreciated my willingness to accurately report what I had found in my assessment even during this difficult time. Eventually, my report was utilized extensively by the Financial Crisis Inquiry Commission ("FCIC") in their work in attempting to understand the causes of the financial crisis. I met with FCIC officials on numerous occasions over a period of months, and eventually testified before the FCIC with regard to my findings in 2008.

Chairman Cox was prescient in telling me that life as Inspector General of the SEC was going to very different than at the Peace Corps. My tenure as Inspector General at the SEC later included several other high-profile investigations, including my investigation of the SEC's failure to uncover Bernie Madoff's $50 billion Ponzi scheme. Operating in the glare of the public eye, while attempting to conduct oversight of the very people with which I was working side-by-side on a daily basis, was tremendously challenging.

Yet, my four-plus years as Inspector General at the SEC were also incredibly rewarding. Moreover, my experiences being in the center of the regulatory storm during the global financial crisis and being in a position to see Congress' reaction firsthand, led me to decide to write this book. As Congress began deliberating what eventually became the Dodd-Frank Wall Street Reform and Consumer Protection Act, I was often asked by congressional officials to provide input and guidance on the legislation. When submitting feedback, I tried to consider how actual companies and compliance officials would be impacted by these regulatory initiatives. I have seen too many occasions when legislation is thought to work well when discussing the proscriptions in theory; but the practical impact was very different.

Now that the Dodd-Frank Act has been enacted and many of the underlying regulations promulgated, I feel it is the responsibility of former government officials like myself to assist companies in responding to the many overlapping regulations that have been put into place. In this book, with the assistance of many very distinguished experts, I have tried to provide detailed, step-by-step guidance for the compliance professional seeking to manage these regulatory responsibilities. The hope is that the information in this book will lead compliance officials and companies to be in a better position to comply fully with their regulatory responsibilities while also achieving both their business and ethical goals and objectives.

Acknowledgments

I want to thank my colleagues at Berkeley Research Group for their helpful comments and edits to the first draft of the book. I wish to mention particularly the contributions of Alexandra Martin and Matthew Caselli. Alex assisted greatly in compiling the information from the interviews that I conducted with the leading experts, and in providing comments and suggestions with respect to all aspects of the book. Matt, as he has done for me on many previous occasions, expertly edited the manuscript and gave me invaluable guidance and direction.

In addition, much, if not most, of the valuable information in the book comes not from me, but from the contributions of the many experts who took the time from their very busy schedules to speak to me and furnish me their insights about the many diverse topics described in the book. These individuals – Amy Lynch, Matt Dwyer, Debbie Monson, Brad Bondi, Richard Roth, Ken McCracken, Jay Knight, and Tom Fox – could not have been more informative or more of a pleasure to work with. It was truly a joy and an honor for me to be able to speak to them about their areas of regulatory expertise, and to be able to incorporate their extremely valuable guidance in this book.

Finally, I am very grateful for the team at John Wiley & Sons, and specifically Thomas Hyrkiel, Tessa Allen and Jeremy Chia. This was a very personal project for me as I was tremendously honored to be able to publish a book for the same publishers for whom my late father, Dr Samuel Kotz, published so many of his books. It was a pleasure to work with Thomas, Tess and Jeremy and I very much appreciated the excitement and dedication that they brought to the project.

About the Author

H. David Kotz (Washington, DC) presently serves as a Managing Director at Berkeley Research Group (BRG), a leading global expert services and consulting firm that provides independent expert testimony, litigation and regulatory support, authoritative studies, strategic advice, and document and data analytics to major law firms, Fortune 500 corporations, government agencies, and regulatory bodies around the world. He is a member of BRG's Capital Markets Practice, where he specializes in the regulation of, and securities trading by, broker-dealers, investment advisers, hedge funds, insurance companies, and banks. He consults with and provides expert testimony on behalf of clients in a wide variety of areas relating to securities fraud, Ponzi schemes, securities market regulation, internal control risk policies, regulations of Futures Commission Merchants, and commodities trading regulation. He also conducts internal investigations and serves as a compliance monitor for firms that have entered into deferred prosecution agreements and similar arrangements with government agencies. Prior to BRG, Kotz served for over four years as the Inspector General of the Securities and Exchange Commission (SEC).

Jurisdiction of Regulators – Who Regulates Whom and What

C ompliance professionals face a myriad of overlapping and confusing regulations and regulators. In the aftermath of the financial crisis, new regulations and increased aggressiveness on the part of regulators have led to growing demands placed on financial firms. The volume and pace of regulatory change has created new and diverse pressures on compliance functions. A primary reason for the overlapping nature of the regulations is that traditionally, financial regulation has evolved through a series of responses to developments and crises in the financial markets. The Dodd-Frank Wall Street Reform and Consumer Protection Act (the "Dodd-Frank" Act), enacted on July 21, 2010, offered some of the most sweeping and comprehensive changes to the financial industry since the Great Depression. The chief impetus for the enactment of the Dodd-Frank Act was the perception that deregulation allowed and encouraged Wall Street to indulge in excesses, resulting in the financial crisis.

Over the years, the financial regulatory system has been modified to address various sources of potential financial instability and attempt to provide regulation and a structure for areas with purported regulatory gaps. With each new crisis, efforts are made to address perceived weaknesses in the regulatory system. The result is a complex regulatory system in which federal Agencies have overlapping jurisdictions. Furthermore, Congress has adopted self-regulation by self-regulatory organizations ("SROs") to prevent excessive government involvement in market operations, and as a more efficient and less expensive way to conduct oversight. However, SRO oversight is, often, in addition to, not instead of, federal regulatory oversight. These structures have resulted in tremendous confusion on the part of compliance professionals whose responsibility it is to make decisions regarding the allocation of often scarce resources to compliance efforts necessitated by the overlapping regulatory schemes.

1.1 FEDERAL FINANCIAL REGULATORY STRUCTURE

The following describes the current federal financial regulatory structure, including the Agencies and the financial institutions they regulate. Federal Agencies regulate banking institutions, securities and futures exchanges, brokers, dealers, mutual funds, and investment advisers. Banking institutions are regulated by several Agencies, led by the Federal Reserve System (commonly referred to as "the Federal Reserve"), which regulates Federal Reserve Bank holding companies, financial holding companies, state banks that are members of the Federal Reserve System, U.S. branches of foreign banks, and foreign branches of U.S. banks.[1] The Office of the Comptroller of the Currency ("OCC") regulates national banks and U.S. federal branches of foreign banks. The Federal Deposit Insurance Corporation ("FDIC") regulates federally-insured depository institutions, including state banks that are not members of the Federal Reserve System.[2] The Office of Thrift Supervision ("OTS") regulates federally chartered and insured thrift institutions and savings and loan holding companies.[3] The National Credit Union Administration ("NCUA") regulates federally-chartered or insured credit unions.[4]

---

[1] For further background on the Federal Reserve System, see the website at www.federalreserve.gov/.

[2] For further background on the FDIC, see the website at www.fdic.gov/.

[3] For further background on the OTS, see the website at www.ots.treas.gov/.

[4] For further background on the NCUA, see the website at http://www.ncua.gov/Pages/default.aspx.

Beyond the banking regulators, the Securities and Exchange Commission ("SEC") regulates securities exchanges and brokers.[5] Lastly, the Commodity Futures Trading Commission ("CFTC") regulates futures exchanges and brokers.[6]

1.2 THE SECURITIES AND EXCHANGE COMMISSION (SEC)

Congress established the SEC in 1934 to enforce the Securities Act of 1933 and the Securities Exchange Act of 1934 (the "Exchange Act").[7] The mission of the SEC is to protect investors; maintain fair, orderly, and efficient markets; and facilitate capital formation.[8] The SEC oversees the key components of the securities world, including securities exchanges, securities brokers and dealers, investment advisers, and mutual funds. The SEC's primary focus is to promote the disclosure of market-related information, maintain fair dealing, and protect against fraud.[9]

Although the SEC is the principal overseer and regulator of the U.S. securities markets, it works closely with the other federal departments and Agencies, self-regulatory organizations, state securities regulators, and various private sector organizations. For example, the Chairman of the SEC works with the Chairman of the Federal Reserve, the Secretary of the Treasury, and the Chairman of the CFTC, and serves as a member of the President's Working Group on Financial Markets.

The SEC is composed of five presidentially-appointed Commissioners, who have staggered five-year terms. By law, no more than three of the Commissioners may belong to the same political party. The Agency's functional responsibilities are organized

---

[5]For further background on the SEC, see the website at www.sec.gov/.

[6]For further background on the CFTC, see the website at http://www.cftc.gov/index.htm.

[7]See Securities Act of 1933 codified at 15 U.S.C. section 77a *et seq.;* Securities Exchange Act of 1934 codified at 15 U.S.C. section 78a *et seq.*

[8]See http://www.sec.gov/about/whatwedo.shtml#.VNOU29hOW70.

[9]See http://www.sec.gov/about/whatwedo.shtml#.VMaC8dhOW70.

into five divisions (Corporation Finance, Trading and Markets, Investment Management, Enforcement, and Economic and Risk Analysis) and 23 offices, headquartered in Washington, D.C.[10]

The SEC's Division of Corporation Finance oversees corporate disclosure of information to the investing public. Corporations are required to comply with regulations pertaining to disclosure that must be made when stock is initially sold and then on a continuing and periodic basis. Corporation Finance (known as "CorpFin") reviews the disclosure documents filed by companies. CorpFin also provides companies with assistance interpreting the Commission's regulations and recommends to the Commission new rules for adoption.[11]

The SEC's Division of Trading and Markets is responsible for maintaining fair, orderly, and efficient markets. Trading and Markets provides day-to-day oversight of the major securities market participants: the securities exchanges; securities firms; self-regulatory organizations; clearing Agencies that help facilitate trade settlement; transfer agents, parties that maintain records of securities owners; securities information processors; and credit rating Agencies. This Division also oversees the Securities Investor Protection Corporation ("SIPC"), which is a private, non-profit corporation that insures the securities and cash in customer accounts of member brokerage firms against the failure of those firms.[12]

The SEC's Division of Investment Management is involved in investor protection and promoting capital formation through oversight and regulation of America's $26 trillion investment management industry. This industry includes mutual funds and the professional fund managers who advise them; analysts who research individual assets and asset classes; and investment advisers to individual customers. Investment Management focuses on ensuring that disclosures about these investments are useful to retail customers,

---

[10]See ibid.

[11]For further background on CorpFin, see the website at http://www.sec.gov/corpfin.

[12]For further background on Trading and Markets, see the website at http://www.sec.gov/tm#.VMaDa9hOW70.

and that the regulatory costs which consumers must bear are not excessive.[13]

The Division of Enforcement is the law enforcement component of the SEC. It recommends the commencement of investigations of securities law violations, whether as civil actions in federal court or as administrative proceedings before an administrative law judge, and prosecutes these cases on behalf of the Commission. Enforcement also works closely with law enforcement Agencies such as the Department of Justice to bring criminal cases. Enforcement obtains evidence of possible violations of the securities laws from many sources, including market surveillance activities, investor tips and complaints, other divisions and offices of the SEC, and the self-regulatory organizations and other securities industry sources.[14]

The SEC's Division of Economic and Risk Analysis (known as "RiskFin") is involved with integrating economic analysis and data analytics into the work of the SEC. RiskFin helps to inform the SEC's policymaking, rulemaking, enforcement, and examinations.[15]

The offices within the SEC include, among others, the Office of the General Counsel, Office of the Chief Accountant, Office of Credit Ratings, Office of International Affairs, Office of Investor Education and Advocacy, and Office of Compliance Inspections and Examinations ("OCIE"). OCIE administers the SEC's examination and inspection program for registered broker-dealers, transfer agents, clearing Agencies, investment companies, and investment advisers. OCIE conducts inspections to foster compliance of the securities laws and to detect violations of the law. When OCIE finds deficiencies, it issues a "deficiency letter" identifying the problems that need to be rectified and monitors the situation until compliance standards are achieved. Violations that are considered serious are referred to the Division of Enforcement. OCIE also examines SROs including national stock exchanges (such as the New York Stock Exchange,

---

[13]For further background on Investment Management, see the website at http://www. sec.gov/investment.

[14]For further background on Enforcement, see the website at http://www.sec.gov/ enforce#.VMaDvdhOW70.

[15]For further background on RiskFin, see the website at http://www.sec.gov/about/ whatwedo.shtml#.VMaDy9hOW73.

NASDAQ, and Chicago Options Board Exchange), registered clearing Agencies, the Municipal Securities Rulemaking Board and the Financial Industry Regulatory Authority ("FINRA").[16]

OCIE oversees FINRA and the other SROs to ensure that they and their members comply with applicable federal securities laws and SRO rules. Consistent with its oversight responsibilities for other SROs, the SEC is responsible for ensuring that FINRA carries out its regulatory responsibilities related to oversight of broker-dealers. The SEC also oversees the adoption of rules and the administration of discipline by SROs such as FINRA. These requirements include that an SRO file a proposed rule change with SEC and publish it on a publicly available website. The SEC then sends a notice of the proposed rule change to the Federal Register and allows interested persons the opportunity to submit written comments concerning the proposed rule change. Concurrently, the SEC reviews the proposed rule change and, if applicable, considers public comments and the SRO's response. The SEC then determines whether the proposed rule change is consistent with the requirements of the applicable statutes and regulations and if appropriate, approves the rule change.

As regulators, SROs, like FINRA, have responsibility for much of the day-to-day oversight of the securities markets and broker-dealers under their jurisdiction. Specifically, SROs are primarily responsible for establishing the standards under which their members conduct business; monitoring the way that business is conducted; and bringing disciplinary actions against their members for violating applicable federal statutes, SEC rules, and their own rules.

1.3   THE FINANCIAL INDUSTRY REGULATORY AUTHORITY (FINRA)

FINRA is the only registered national securities association and has regulatory oversight of all securities broker-dealers doing business with the public in the United States. FINRA's mission is to safeguard the investing public against fraud and bad practices. All brokers must

---

[16]For further background on OCIE, see the website at http://www.sec.gov/ocie# .VMaEBdhOW70.

be licensed and registered by FINRA, pass qualification exams, and satisfy continuing education requirements. FINRA conducts routine examinations, as well as inquiries based on investor complaints and suspicious activity. It also reviews all broker advertisements, websites, sales brochures, and other communications to make sure brokers present information in a fair and balanced manner. FINRA also monitors trading in the U.S. stock markets.[17]

FINRA has an enforcement program that brings discipline where it believes that investors have been harmed. FINRA investigations are non-public and confidential, and firms and individuals are entitled to be represented by counsel. To conduct its investigations, FINRA requests documents and takes sworn testimony from firms and associated persons. FINRA may also contact customers and other individuals who are not within FINRA's jurisdiction to learn about the member firms' activities and who may provide information voluntarily to FINRA. FINRA then analyzes the evidence it obtained, reviews the applicable law, and makes a preliminary determination of whether or not a violation appears to have occurred. If FINRA determines that rules have been violated, it will resolve whether the conduct merits a recommendation of formal disciplinary action. If the violation is of a minor nature where there is an absence of customer harm or detrimental market impact, the matter may be settled with an informal disciplinary action. Otherwise, FINRA will proceed through a more formal route by commencing a full-blown Enforcement proceeding. In 2014, FINRA brought 1,397 disciplinary actions against registered individuals and firms, levied fines totaling more than $134 million, and ordered restitution of more than $32.3 million to harmed investors.[18]

FINRA also provides investor education through the implementation of programs like BrokerCheck, which gives investors a quick way to check a broker's disciplinary and professional background. In FINRA's Market Data Center, investors can find information and data on equities, options, bonds, and mutual funds.[19] FINRA's

---

[17] For further background on FINRA, see the website at www.finra.org/.

[18] See http://www.finra.org/AboutFINRA/WhatWeDo/.

[19] For further information on FINRA's Market Data Center, see http://finra-markets.morningstar.com/MarketData/Default.jsp.

Trade Reporting and Compliance Engine ("TRACE") system helps investors monitor their bond investments by providing them with timely and accurate pricing information for corporate and Agency bonds.[20] FINRA also has a dispute resolution forum, which is the largest in the country for the securities industry, handling nearly 100 percent of securities-related arbitrations and mediations from more than 70 hearing locations – including at least one in all 50 states, London, and Puerto Rico.[21]

1.4   THE COMMODITY FUTURES TRADING COMMISSION (CFTC)

The SEC's counterpart for futures exchanges and brokers is the CFTC. The CFTC is an independent Agency of the United States government that regulates futures and options markets. The stated mission of the CFTC is "to protect market participants and the public from fraud, manipulation, abusive practices, and systemic risk related to derivatives – both futures and swaps – and to foster transparent, open, competitive and financially sound markets."[22] The CFTC states that it carries out this mission by "polic[ing] the derivatives markets for various abuses and works to ensure the protection of customer funds."[23]

In carrying out this mission, the CFTC polices the derivatives markets for various abuses and works to ensure the protection of customer funds. The CFTC also oversees designated contract markets, swap execution facilities, derivatives clearing organizations, swap data repositories, swap dealers, futures commission merchants, commodity pool operators, and other intermediaries.

The CFTC is composed of three major divisions: Market Oversight, Clearing and Intermediary Oversight, and Enforcement. The

---

[20]For further information on FINRA's TRACE system, see http://www.finra.org/Industry/Compliance/MarketTransparency/TRACE/.

[21]For further information on FINRA's Dispute Resolution programs, see http://www.finra.org/ArbitrationAndMediation/FINRADisputeResolution/.

[22]See http://www.cftc.gov/About/MissionResponsibilities/index.htm.

[23]See ibid.

CFTC's Division of Market Oversight ensures that the futures markets are operating efficiently without manipulation and fraud. These tasks are executed first by reviewing and analyzing the very diverse group of instruments and products to ensure that they are not susceptible to manipulation. Market Oversight also conducts active market and trade practice surveillance of trading activity on designated contract markets (known as "DCMs"), like the New York Mercantile Exchange. Traders establishing positions on DCMs are subject to reporting requirements so the CFTC can evaluate position sizes to detect and deter manipulation. Market Oversight monitors the activities of large traders, key price relationships, and relevant supply and demand factors for the estimated 1,400 active futures and option contracts in the country to ensure market integrity. In addition, CFTC surveillance economists prepare weekly summary reports for futures and option contracts approaching their expiration periods.

The CFTC's Division of Clearing and Intermediary Oversight ensures the financial integrity of transactions on the markets regulated by the CFTC. This division attempts to establish that the intermediaries managing these funds are properly registered, perform appropriate recordkeeping, have adequate capital, employ fair sales practices, and protect the funds their customers invest. Intermediaries overseen by the CFTC include futures commission merchants ("FCMS"), including banks and broker-dealers with specialized futures operations, as well as stand-alone futures trading houses.[24]

The CFTC's Division of Enforcement investigates and prosecutes violations of the federal laws governing commodity trading by individuals and firms who are engaged in activities that directly or indirectly affect commodity futures and option trading on domestic exchanges. These federal laws prohibit fraud and abusive practices in solicitations of futures or options, such as falsely guaranteeing profits, minimizing risk, and misrepresenting performance history. In addition, the CFTC is authorized to bring enforcement actions

---

[24]For further background on the CFTC's Division of Clearing and Intermediary Oversight, see http://www.cftc.gov/About/CFTCOrganization/index.htm.

for misappropriating customer funds, and often refers matters to criminal authorities.[25]

The CFTC administers the Commodity Exchange Act ("CEA"), 7 U.S.C. section 1 *et seq.*, which prohibits fraudulent conduct in the trading of futures contracts. The CEA also establishes a comprehensive regulatory structure to oversee the volatile futures trading markets. The CEA requires all FCMs to register with the CFTC, unless they qualify for a particular exemption.[26] CFTC regulations promulgated pursuant to the CEA also require all registered FCMs to be a member of a Futures Association.[27]

1.5   THE NATIONAL FUTURES ASSOCIATION (NFA)

The National Futures Association ("NFA") is the industry-wide, self-regulatory organization for the U.S. futures industry and the "designated" regulatory organization for non-clearing FCMs.[28] The NFA screens all firms and individuals wishing to register with the CFTC and become members of the NFA. Applicants must meet fitness requirements to determine if they have ever been disciplined or subject to regulatory proceedings in the past, and must provide fingerprint cards for Federal Bureau of Investigation ("FBI") background checks. In addition, individual registrants must pass proficiency testing requirements. The NFA has the authority to deny, revoke, suspend, restrict, or condition the registration of any firm or individual.

The NFA has adopted a comprehensive set of rules covering the business conduct of its members, including sales practices, record-keeping, reporting, risk disclosure, discretionary trading, disclosure of fees, and minimum capital requirements.

Pursuant to its examination or audit program, the NFA is required to examine FCMs on an annual basis if they hold customer funds.[29]

---

[25]For further background on the CFTC's Division of Enforcement, see http://www.cftc.gov/LawRegulation/Enforcement/index.htm.

[26]See 7 U.S.C. section 6d(a).

[27]See CFTC Regulation 170.15.

[28]For further background on FINRA, see www.nfa.futures.org/.

[29]See http://www.nfa.futures.org/NFA-faqs/compliance-faqs/examinations/index.HTML.

As part of these examinations or audits, the NFA examination may include all the FCM's procedures, books, and records associated with its commodities business, including, but not limited to:[30]

- Corporate records.
- Anti-money laundering policies and practices.
- Sales practices.
- Supervisory procedures.
- Account opening documents.
- Order tickets.
- Bunched order allocations.
- Margin policies.
- Promotional material.
- Disclosure documents.
- Performance capsule support.
- Bank records.
- Trading records.
- Financial statement records.

In addition, the NFA has the authority to take disciplinary actions against any firm or individual that violates its rules. These actions range from Warning Letters for minor rule infractions to formal complaints in cases where rule violations warrant prosecution. Penalties resulting from complaints include expulsion, suspension for a fixed period, prohibition from future association with any NFA Member, censure, reprimand, and a fine of up to $250,000 per violation. The NFA often collaborates with the CFTC, and other law enforcement Agencies to ensure full, comprehensive prosecutions.[31]

The NFA has also worked closely with the CFTC and other SROs to adopt a number of initiatives to further safeguard customer funds. The NFA, in conjunction with other SROs, developed and implemented a system in 2013 that requires all depositories holding customer segregated funds on behalf of an FCM

---

[30] See ibid.

[31] See http://www.nfa.futures.org/NFA-about-nfa/who-we-are/how-NFA-fights-fraud-and-abuse.HTML.

to directly report balances daily to SROs. The SROs then perform an automated comparison to the daily reports filed by the FCMs to identify any suspicious discrepancies. In addition, each FCM is required to provide regulators with immediate notification if it draws down its excess segregated funds (funds deposited by the firm into customer segregated accounts to guard against customer defaults) by 25 percent in any given day. Such withdrawals must be approved by the Chief Executive Officer ("CEO"), Chief Financial Officer ("CFO") or a financial principal of the firm, and the principal must certify that the firm remains in compliance with segregation requirements.[32]

All FCMs also must regularly file certain financial information about the firm with the NFA. This information is posted on the NFA's website. The information includes each FCM's capital requirement, excess capital, segregated funds requirement, excess segregated funds, and how the firm invests customer segregated funds.[33]

The NFA also began an arbitration program in 1983, providing a method for investors to resolve futures-related disputes. Since that time, NFA arbitration has become the primary venue for dispute resolution for retail futures and foreign exchange ("forex") customers. The NFA also offers a mediation alternative during the arbitration process in cases where the total amount of the arbitration claim is $150,000 or less.[34]

1.6   THE DEPARTMENT OF JUSTICE (DOJ)

As noted above, these regulatory entities coordinate as appropriate with the Department of Justice ("DOJ"). The DOJ is a federal

---

[32] See   http://www.nfa.futures.org/NFA-about-nfa/who-we-are/customer-protection-initiat ives.HTML.

[33] See ibid.

[34] Mediation is a settlement process in which the parties work together with a mediator to find a mutually agreeable solution. For further information on the NFA's arbitration programs, see http://www.nfa.futures.org/%5C/NFA-about-nfa/who-we-are/dispute-resolution.HTML.

department designed to enforce the law and defend the interests of the United States.[35] The mission of the DOJ is to:

> *enforce the law and defend the interests of the United States according to the law; to ensure public safety against threats foreign and domestic; to provide federal leadership in preventing and controlling crime; to seek just punishment for those guilty of unlawful behavior; and to ensure fair and impartial administration of justice for all Americans.*[36]

Offices and groups within the U.S. Department of Justice include the Federal Bureau of Investigation, the Drug Enforcement Administration, the Bureau of Prisons, the U.S. Federal Marshals, and the U.S. Parole Commission. The SEC and CFTC coordinate with the DOJ on enforcement cases, as they often initiate civil proceedings against the same actors or involving similar facts to criminal proceedings brought by the DOJ.

In addition, the DOJ and SEC share enforcement authority for the anti-bribery and accounting provisions of the Federal Corrupt Practices Act ("FCPA"). The DOJ has criminal FCPA enforcement authority over "issuers" (i.e., public companies) and their officers, directors, employees, agents, or stockholders acting on the issuer's behalf. The DOJ also has both criminal and civil enforcement responsibility for the FCPA's anti-bribery provisions over "domestic concerns" – including (a) U.S. citizens, nationals, and residents, and (b) U.S. businesses and their officers, directors, employees, agents, or stockholders acting on the domestic concern's behalf – and certain foreign persons and businesses that act in furtherance of an FCPA violation while in the territory of the United States. The SEC is responsible for civil enforcement of the FCPA over issuers and their officers, directors, employees, agents, or stockholders acting on the issuer's behalf.[37] The SEC, CFTC, FINRA, and NFA all refer potential criminal matters to the DOJ for prosecution.

---

[35] For further background on the DOJ, see the website at www.justice.gov/.
[36] http://www.justice.gov/about/.
[37] See http://www.justice.gov/criminal/fraud/fcpa/guidance/guide.pdf.

1.7   RECENT REGULATORY FAILURES TO UNCOVER FRAUD

Notwithstanding the resources and efforts made by the federal Agencies and SROs to protect investors from fraud in the securities and futures markets, these Agencies and SROs have failed over the past few years to uncover several large frauds that have caused extraordinary harm to thousands of investors. In my role as Inspector General of the SEC for over four years from late 2007 until early 2012, I investigated several of these failures.

In December 2008, I conducted an investigation of how the SEC failed to uncover Bernie Madoff's $50 billion Ponzi scheme. When I began the investigation, I knew the SEC had been provided with several complaints and tips about Madoff's extraordinarily consistent returns and accusations that he may have been perpetrating a fraud. As a result, I thought, like many others, that these complaints had likely fallen through the cracks. I knew that government Agencies receive thousands of complaints every year and I began to sympathize with the possibility that SEC officials simply missed the import of these complaints. But in my investigation, I learned that the SEC had, in fact, conducted examinations and investigations of many of the tips and complaints they received; they simply failed to conduct competent exams or investigations. My investigation found that between June 1992 and December 2008, the SEC received six substantive complaints that raised significant red flags concerning Madoff's hedge fund operations and should have led to questions about whether Madoff was actually engaged in trading. In addition, the SEC conducted two investigations and three examinations related to Madoff's investment advisory business based upon the detailed and credible complaints that they received.[38]

The SEC failed to uncover Madoff's Ponzi scheme for several reasons, including a lack of experience and expertise on the part of the SEC investigators and examiners; Madoff's personal reputation

---

[38]See *Investigation of the SEC to Uncover Bernard Madoff's Ponzi Scheme*, SEC Office of Inspector General, Report No. OIG-509, August 31, 2009 at http://www.sec.gov/news/studies/2009/oig-509.pdf.

and ability to impress and manipulate the SEC investigators and examiners; and a lack of follow-up on the part of SEC investigators and examiners who, in many cases, began taking the correct (and relatively easy) steps to uncover the fraud, but failed to follow through.

Not long after issuing the Madoff report, I investigated another fraud, perpetrated by a Texan named Allen Stanford, which the SEC eventually uncovered after Madoff confessed in 2009, but which the SEC knew about for many years and took very limited action on, notwithstanding such awareness of Stanford's questionable investments. Stanford had been registered as both an investment adviser and broker-dealer in Texas and was affiliated with an offshore investment bank in Antigua. The Antiguan bank evidently offered Stanford's customers Certificate of Deposit ("CD") accounts with relatively high and very steady interest rates.

My investigation found that the SEC's Fort Worth office had been aware, since 1997, that Stanford was likely operating a Ponzi scheme, having come to that conclusion a mere two years after Stanford Group Company, Stanford's investment adviser, registered with the SEC in 1995. Over the next eight years, the SEC's Fort Worth Examination group conducted four examinations of Stanford's operations, finding in each examination that the CDs could not have been "legitimate," and that it was "highly unlikely" that the returns Stanford claimed to generate could have been achieved with the purported conservative investment approach. Fort Worth examiners dutifully conducted examinations of Stanford in 1997, 1998, 2002, and 2004, concluding in each case that Stanford's CDs were likely a Ponzi scheme or a similar fraudulent scheme.[39]

The problem was not with the SEC's Examination group, but with Enforcement in Fort Worth. The Examination group had tried for years to get Enforcement to investigate Stanford but was, for the most part, unsuccessful. The primary reason for this lack of success was that the former head of Enforcement in Fort Worth, an attorney

---

[39] See *Investigation of the SEC's Response to Concerns Regarding Robert Allen Stanford's Alleged Ponzi Scheme*, SEC Office of Inspector General, Report No. OIG-526, March 31 2010 at http://www.sec.gov/news/studies/2010/oig-526.pdf.

named Spencer Barasch, had pushed back against bringing an action against Stanford on the ground that the case was too complex and difficult. Ironically, when Barasch left the SEC, he sought to represent Stanford on three separate occasions, and in fact represented Stanford briefly in 2006 before he was informed by the SEC Ethics Office that it was improper to do so.

The reluctance of Barasch and others to bring the Stanford case related to larger institutional influences operating within the SEC at that time. The Fort Worth Enforcement officials perceived that they were being judged on the numbers of cases they brought, so-called "stats," and communicated to the Enforcement staff that novel or complex cases were disfavored. As a result, cases like Stanford, which were not considered "quick-hit" or "slam-dunk" cases, were not encouraged.

An internal FINRA investigation also disclosed that it was not merely the SEC that failed to uncover the Madoff and Stanford frauds. According to a report issued by a Special Review Committee retained by FINRA in September 2009, FINRA staff had conducted examinations of both Madoff and Stanford. The report also disclosed that between 2003 and 2005, the National Association of Securities Dealers – FINRA's predecessor entity – received credible information from at least five different sources claiming that the Stanford CDs were a potential fraud. The internal investigation concluded that FINRA missed a number of opportunities to investigate the Stanford firm's role in the CD scheme. Even though the investigation did not uncover evidence that FINRA received whistleblower complaints regarding the Madoff scheme or that the SEC shared any concerns or specific allegations about Madoff with FINRA, it did find that the SEC in 2006 had caused the Madoff firm to register as an investment adviser and to submit information on its advisory business to a system operated by FINRA pursuant to a contract with the SEC. In the course of their cycle examinations, FINRA examiners did come across several facts worthy of inquiry associated with the Madoff scheme that should have been pursued. The report particularly noted that the Madoff case highlighted the need to improve the exchange of information within FINRA and between the SEC and FINRA, including the sharing of information about potentially fraudulent conduct at member firms.[40]

In addition, the recent record of the CFTC and the NFA could be improved with respect to large frauds. After I had left the SEC, my consulting firm, Berkeley Research Group, was retained to conduct an investigation of why the regulators were unable to uncover a fraud perpetrated by Russell Wasendorf, the Chairman and CEO of Peregrine Financial Group ("PFG"), an Iowa-based FCM that had operated for more than 20 years.

In July 2012, the FBI discovered multiple copies of a lengthy, confessional statement signed by Wasendorf, describing how he perpetrated a nearly 20-year fraud by forging bank account records. In this statement, Wasendorf outlined how, through a scheme of using false bank statements, he embezzled millions of dollars from customer accounts at PFG. Wasendorf concealed the fraud by having bank statements delivered to himself and making counterfeit statements within a few hours of receiving the actual statements using a combination of Photoshop, Excel, scanners, and both laser and ink jet printers. Wasendorf provided these forgeries to his firm's accounting department, his external auditor, and the regulators. When the regulators and auditors would request bank information and statements, Wasendorf would put a fake P.O. Box address on the counterfeit bank statements. When the auditors mailed the forms to the bank's false address, Wasendorf would intercept the forms, type in the amount of money that was supposed to be in the account, forge a bank officer's signature, and mail it back to the regulator or auditor.

In the investigation, we learned that the NFA had conducted 27 audits of PFG during the period 1995 to 2012. These audits included 17 unannounced annual audits conducted every nine to 15 months, seven audits of PFG's branch offices, an additional audit during 2010, and two additional audits in 2011. We also discovered that the CFTC conducted several reviews of PFG over the years but failed

---

[40]See *Report of the 2009 Special Review Committee on FINRA's Examination Program in light of the Stanford and Madoff Schemes*, FINRA Special Review Committee, September 2009, at http://www.finra.org/web/groups/corporate/@corp/documents/corporate/p120078.pdf.

to uncover the fraud. According to Wasendorf, in fact, the CFTC audited his firm five times during a six-month period circa 1994. On one occasion, a senior-level CFTC official attempted to obtain signed bank confirmations directly from Wasendorf's bank but did not exert sufficient pressure on the bank to obtain the documentation.[41]

On one occasion, the NFA came close to uncovering Wasendorf's fraud. In nearly all of the NFA's audits of PFG, NFA auditors received bank confirmations in the mail showing the same balance as in the firm's financial statements because Wasendorf would intercept the NFA bank confirmation request sent in the mail, and provide counterfeit statements back to the NFA that would match his firm's records.

In 2011, however, the field supervisor for the 2011 NFA audit of PFG had heard that they were having a hard time getting confirmations back through the mail and NFA auditors asked the PFG's Director of Compliance to reach out directly to the banks to obtain the information. As a result of this request, PFG's Compliance Director e-mailed the NFA's bank confirmations to her bank contacts. That same day, the bank officer sent the filled out confirmation forms back to PFG's Compliance Director and the NFA auditor. The balance reflected on the bank confirmation for the Peregrine Financial Group customer account was approximately $7 million. By contrast, the bank statements that the NFA auditors reviewed from Wasendorf's firm records showed a balance in the customer accounts of over $218 million. Thus, there was a $211 million discrepancy between the amount of money that Wasendorf's firm claimed was in its customer accounts, and the actual amount of money in these accounts. Notwithstanding this discrepancy, which was noticed by an NFA staff auditor, no action was initially taken as a result.[42]

On the next business day after the NFA received the correct confirmation directly from the bank, Wasendorf prepared a forged confirmation bank statement, and faxed the forged statement to the

---

[41] See *Analysis of the National Futures Association's Audits of Peregrine Financial Group, Inc.*, Berkeley Research Group, January 29, 2013, at http://www.nfa.futures.org/news/BRG/report_of_investigation.pdf.
[42] See ibid.

NFA pretending to be from the bank, with a note that said: "Attached please find a corrected copy of the Bank Balance Confirmation for the Peregrine Financial Group" customer account. The bank confirmation attached to the facsimile cover sheet showed a balance of over $218 million. The NFA auditor accepted the "corrected" confirmation and there was no follow-up with respect to the previous confirmation received or the discrepancy.[43]

As a result of these high-profile failures, there have been improvements in the SEC, CFTC, FINRA, and the NFA with respect to their operations and these entities are, hopefully, in a better position to detect fraud today. In each of the investigations, with which I was personally involved, my SEC or BRG colleagues and I provided numerous specific and concrete recommendations in an attempt to remedy the deficiencies that we found led to the failures. In all of these cases, we made sure that the Agencies implemented our recommendations.

1.8 EXPERT ADVICE ON OVERLAPPING REGULATIONS

Regardless of the ability of regulators to uncover fraud and perform their duties and obligations, companies remain subject to their overlapping oversight and supervision. In addition, as a result of the financial crisis, new regulatory responsibilities have been promulgated by the Dodd-Frank Act, and regulators are more aggressive than ever in enforcing the myriad of rules and regulations. Each regulator conducts its examinations and investigations in its own unique way, and having an understanding of the motivations and approaches of each regulator is critical to effectively managing the regulatory burdens.

The following chapters provide "one-stop shopping" for compliance professionals to manage the regulatory process and include specific and hands-on advice from myself and expert industry leaders on regulatory and compliance-related topics.

---

[43] See ibid.

Chapter 2 describes how companies can cultivate an ethical culture, create effective policies and procedures, and ensure accountability within an organization, with an emphasis on the new compliance rules and procedures enacted as a result of the Dodd-Frank Act.

Chapter 3 provides practical advice for companies with regard to managing whistleblower complaints and a detailed description of the whistleblower offices at both the SEC and CFTC, and describes how companies can implement policies and procedures that can limit their exposure from internal complaints.

Chapter 4 describes how firms can defend and manage examinations conducted by SEC's OCIE of financial firms and includes advice and guidance from industry expert, Amy Lynch, who has over 20 years of experience in the financial industry, and has conducted examinations for OCIE in the SEC's New York and Washington, D.C. offices. She also advises firms on how to defend these exams as President of a compliance-based consulting firm.

Chapter 5 discusses how firms can defend FINRA examinations with expertise and guidance included from industry expert Matt Dwyer, who served as a Senior Compliance Examiner at FINRA for six years before starting a consulting firm that advises firms subject to FINRA's jurisdiction on defending examinations and fulfilling their regulatory obligations.

Chapter 6 describes how firms can manage and defend NFA examinations and includes the thoughts and perspectives of industry expert, Deborah Monson, a partner at the law firm of Ropes & Gray, who focuses on commodities law, asset management, and private investment funds and has represented entities subject to NFA jurisdiction for many years.

Chapter 7 provides advice and guidance to companies who may be subject to an SEC investigation and/or Enforcement action, incorporating the perspective of industry expert, Bradley J. Bondi, a partner and the leader of the Securities Enforcement practice at the law firm of Cahill Gordon & Reindel in Washington, D.C., and a recognized expert in SEC Enforcement cases, who served as counsel to two SEC Commissioners.

Chapter 8 describes how companies can defend Enforcement actions brought by FINRA, with special guidance from industry expert, Richard A. Roth, founder and partner of the Roth Law Firm, who defends companies and serves as an arbitrator in FINRA Enforcement proceedings.

Chapter 9 focuses on CFTC Enforcement actions and includes advice and guidance from Kenneth W. McCracken, a former Chief Trial Attorney in the CFTC's Division of Enforcement, and a partner at the law firm of Schiff Hardin LLP, where he represents individuals and companies in investigations and defending actions brought by the CFTC. Chapter 10 discusses how companies can defend themselves in NFA Enforcement proceedings and provides the unique perspective of Ronald Hirst, the current Associate General Counsel/Enforcement Coordinator for the NFA.

Chapter 11 describes how firms can participate in the regulatory rulemaking process and incorporates guidance from industry expert, Jay Knight, a partner in the law firm of Bass, Berry & Sims, whose law practice includes counseling companies on regulatory reporting matters. Knight also previously held several positions in the SEC's Division of Corporation Finance, including as a member of the SEC Dodd-Frank Implementation Team, where he led a team of attorneys, economists, and accountants charged with implementing rulemaking projects under the Dodd-Frank Act.

Chapter 12 deals with how companies can defend claims brought under the FCPA and includes advice from industry expert, Thomas Fox, an author of eight books on the FCPA and compliance, who has practiced law in Houston for 30 years assisting companies with FCPA compliance programs.

Chapter 13 provides practical advice on how to conduct comprehensive and thorough internal investigations and includes strategies and techniques on how to obtain information and limit exposure from the regulatory Agencies as a result of the allegations that led to the investigation.

Finally, Chapter 14 provides perspective on the regulatory climate post-financial crisis and critiques the federal government's efforts to reduce duplicative and overlapping regulations. All of these chapters include my own perspectives and lessons learned from my years in the financial public and private sectors. The chapters also incorporate many fascinating stories and anecdotes from the high-profile investigations I conducted while serving as the IG of the SEC during the financial crisis.

CHAPTER 2

How to Strengthen Governance and Compliance in Light of New Regulations

C orporate governance refers to the set of policies, principles, and processes by which a company is governed. These provide the guidelines as to how a company can be controlled and directed. Corporate governance involves a set of relationships between a company's management, its board, its shareholders, and other stakeholders. The most important principles associated with good corporate governance include conducting business with integrity, complying with the applicable rules and regulations, demonstrating responsibility and accountability toward stakeholders, and achieving transparency in connection with company decisions. Good corporate governance can improve a company's reputation, engender confidence in its leadership, encourage investment, and positively impact its share price.

In order to achieve good corporate governance, companies must have in place effective controls and risk management processes to identify potential deficiencies and failures and provide for overall monitoring of corporate activities. Through risk management, companies identify, assess, and prioritize all kinds of risk. Once this is accomplished, a plan is created to minimize or eliminate the impact of a negative event.

After joining the SEC as its Inspector General in December 2007, I conducted one of the first assessments of the causes of the financial crisis. On September 25, 2008, my office issued a comprehensive audit report analyzing the SEC's oversight of Consolidated Supervised Entities ("CSEs").[1] The CSE program was a voluntary program created by the SEC in 2004, to allow the SEC to supervise certain broker-dealer holding companies on a consolidated basis. These entities included Bear Stearns, Lehman Brothers, Goldman Sachs, Morgan Stanley, Merrill Lynch, Citigroup Inc. and JP Morgan. Our audit focused primarily on the circumstances leading up to the collapse of Bear Stearns in March 2008.

In the audit, we found evidence of significant shortcomings in the area of risk management at Bear Stearns, including a lack of expertise by Bear Stearns risk managers in mortgage-backed securities at various times, lack of timely formal review by Bear Stearns' risk managers of mortgage models, persistent understaffing in Bear Stearns' risk department, proximity of Bear Stearns' risk managers to traders suggesting a lack of independence, turnover of key risk personnel during times of crisis, and the inability or unwillingness of Bear Stearns' risk managers to update models to reflect changing circumstances.

For example, the audit found that in 2006, the expertise of Bear Stearns' risk managers was focused on pricing exotic derivatives and validating derivatives models. At the same time, Bear Stearns' business was becoming increasingly concentrated in mortgage securities, an area in which its model review still needed much work. Overall, we concluded that at that time, the risk managers at Bear Stearns did not have the skill sets that best matched Bear Stearns' business model and were not engaged in the proper modeling.

Similarly, in the Final Report of the National Commission on the Causes of the Financial and Economic Crisis in the United States prepared by the Financial Crisis Inquiry Commission ("FCIC") in January 2011, the FCIC concluded that the financial crisis was the result of the failure of financial institutions to question, understand,

---

[1] See *SEC's Oversight of Bear Stearns and Related Entities: The Consolidated Supervised Entity Program*, SEC Office of Inspector General, Report No. 446-A, September 25, 2008, at http://www.sec.gov/about/oig/audit/2008/446-a.pdf.

and manage evolving risks within a system essential to the well-being of the American public.[2] The FCIC also found that dramatic failures of corporate governance and risk management at many systemically important financial institutions were a key cause of the crisis.

The FCIC's examination further revealed what they described as "stunning instances of governance breakdowns and irresponsibility," providing examples such as AIG senior management's ignorance of the terms and risks of the company's $79 billion derivatives exposure to mortgage-related securities, Fannie Mae's quest for bigger market share, profits, and bonuses, which led it to ramp up its exposure to risky loans and securities as the housing market was peaking, and Merrill Lynch's top management last-minute realization that the company held $55 billion in supposedly "super-safe" mortgage-related securities that resulted in billions of dollars in losses.

Concerns about corporate governance and responsibility and risk management were significant factors in the enactment of the Dodd-Frank Act. At the Dodd-Frank Act signing ceremony, President Obama stated:

> *While a number of factors led to such a severe recession, the primary cause was a breakdown in our financial system. It was a crisis born of a failure of responsibility from certain corners of Wall Street to the halls of power in Washington. For years, our financial sector was governed by antiquated and poorly enforced rules that allowed some to game the system and take risks that endangered the entire economy.*[3]

2.1 DODD-FRANK ACT'S IMPACT ON GOVERNANCE AND COMPLIANCE

In addition to providing sweeping changes to the financial regulatory landscape, the Dodd-Frank Act included several specific provisions

---

[2]See *Final Report of the National Commission on the Causes of the Financial and Economic Crisis in the United States*, Financial Crisis Inquiry Commission, January 2011 at http://www.gpo.gov/fdsys/pkg/GPO-FCIC/pdf/GPO-FCIC.pdf.

[3]See *Remarks by the President at Signing of Dodd-Frank Wall Street Reform and Consumer Protection Act*, July 21, 2010, at http://www.whitehouse.gov/the-press-office/remarks-president-signing-dodd-frank-wall-street-reform-and-consumer-protection-act.

relating to governance and compliance. In the area of corporate governance, the Dodd-Frank Act contained provisions relating to: (a) shareholder advisory votes on executive compensation and golden parachutes; (b) limitations on discretionary voting by brokers; (c) clawbacks of incentive compensation; (d) independence of compensation committees; (e) enhanced proxy disclosures; (f) whistleblower incentives and protection; and (g) proxy access.

However, one can address the specific corporate governance changes and rules in the Dodd-Frank Act in much the same manner that one should address the myriad of compliance and regulatory challenges – by creating effective policies, strengthening accountability through the company, and establishing and maintaining an ethical culture.

An example of one such change is section 951 of the Dodd-Frank Act that added section 14A to the Exchange Act, which requires companies, among other things, to periodically conduct separate shareholder advisory votes to approve the compensation of certain executive officers.[4] Section 14A also requires companies soliciting votes to approve a merger or acquisition to disclose any "golden parachute" arrangements and, in certain circumstances, conduct a separate shareholder advisory vote to approve these arrangements. Similarly, section 957 of the Dodd-Frank Act amended section 6(b) of the Exchange Act to provide that national securities exchanges must prohibit brokers from voting shares they do not beneficially own in connection with the election of directors, executive compensation, and any other significant matter, as determined by the SEC, unless the beneficial owner of the security has instructed the broker on how to vote.[5]

One of the best methods to ensure compliance with both section 14A and the amended section 6(b) of the Exchange Act is to establish well-thought-out voting guidelines of proxy advisers and key shareholders and ensure that the company's compensation policies and practices conform to those guidelines. In addition, one should

---

[4]See section 951 of Pub. L. No. 111-203 (July 21, 2010).
[5]See ibid., section 957.

review golden parachute arrangements to ensure that the terms are appropriate and suitable for public viewing and voting.

In another development, section 954 of the Dodd-Frank Act added section 10D to the Exchange Act, which directs the SEC to adopt rules prohibiting a national securities exchange or association from listing a company unless it develops, implements, and discloses a policy regarding the recovery of executive compensation in the event of an accounting restatement due to material noncompliance with a financial reporting requirement.[6] In addition, section 952 of the Dodd-Frank Act added section 10C to the Exchange Act, which directs the SEC to adopt rules prohibiting a national securities exchange or association from listing a company that does not comply with certain newly enacted independence requirements. These requirements include that each compensation committee member must be considered an "independent" director (as defined by the SEC) and that the committees have authority to engage, and be directly responsible for the appointment, compensation, and oversight of the work of independent compensation consultants, legal counsel, or other advisors to the compensation committee. Section 952 lists various "independence" factors for the SEC to consider.[7]

Furthermore, section 953 of the Dodd-Frank Act added section 14(i) to the Exchange Act, which directs the SEC to adopt rules requiring disclosure in the proxy material for an annual meeting of information that shows the relationship between executive compensation actually paid and the financial performance of the company, taking into account any change in the value of stock, dividends, and distributions.[8] Section 953 also directed the SEC to amend Item 402 of Regulation S-K to require disclosure of (1) the median of the annual total compensation of all employees except the CEO; (2) the annual total compensation of the CEO; and (3) the ratio of the amount described in clause (1) to the amount described in clause (2).[9] Responding effectively to these new provisions will involve

---

[6] See ibid., section 954.
[7] See ibid., section 952.
[8] See ibid., section 953.
[9] See ibid., section 953.

identifying appropriate metrics to measure pay for performance adequately, and creating a compensation philosophy and advocating compensation decisions based upon best practices, which can then be justified and presented to shareholders.

Further, section 922 of the Dodd-Frank Act added section 21F to the Exchange Act, which requires the SEC to pay an award to an eligible whistleblower who voluntarily provides the SEC with original information about a violation of the federal securities laws that leads to a successful action resulting in monetary sanctions exceeding $1 million.[10] The amount of the award is between 10 percent and 30 percent of the monetary sanctions collected in connection with the action and certain related actions. The SEC will determine the award in its discretion after considering, among other factors, the significance of the information and the degree of assistance provided by the whistleblower. Section 21F also expanded the protections available to whistleblowers and provides whistleblowers who have been subject to retaliation with a private right of action.[11] These provisions will likely lead to more whistleblowers coming forward, which companies may address by evaluating their internal processes for dealing with whistleblowers and strengthening their overall internal compliance programs and commitment to ethical conduct.[12]

Finally, section 971 of the Dodd-Frank Act amended section 14(a) of the Exchange Act to expressly authorize the SEC to issue rules requiring a company's proxy solicitation materials to include a director nominee submitted by a shareholder.[13] Responding to this provision will require effective shareholder communication and ensuring that shareholder concerns are addressed and resolved as quickly and thoroughly as possible.

---

[10] See ibid., section 922.

[11] See ibid., section 922.

[12] For a more detailed discussion of how to manage the SEC's revised whistleblower program, see Chapter 3, entitled, "How to Manage Whistleblowers' Complaints."

[13] See section 971 of Pub. L. No. 111-203 (July 21, 2010).

2.2 MANAGING EXECUTIVE COMPENSATION

Executive compensation issues have been the subject of much debate in recent years, and how companies deal with these issues can be significant in terms of corporate governance and establishing an ethical culture in the workplace. This can also be a very divisive issue and lead to disputes with shareholder groups that can cause dissension within a company. Companies have the ability to anticipate and forestall these disputes without the necessity of dictating limitations on the amount of money earned by top executives, but by dealing with the concept of executive compensation in a fair and transparent manner.

The first step in this process is to ensure full and complete disclosure of the true and accurate compensation being paid to an executive. One should ensure that any hidden payouts be fully disclosed so that shareholders or employees will not get the impression that compensation is being concealed from them.

Second, one should make efforts to tie the executives' pay to performance such as returns given to shareholders or the company's profit levels. Moreover, the pay should be related to both long- and short-term goals, so that executives are not incentivized to take short-term actions favorable to their bottom line, but not the company's long-term health. For example, one can pay a larger percentage of compensation with restricted stock that must be held for several years. In addition, clawback provisions may be established to enable companies to recover compensation from executives who have been shown to damage the company through misconduct.

Third, offering stock options to employees is a good way of developing an ownership culture within a firm, particularly when the options are conditioned on a firm's profit levels. If employees view themselves as in the same situation as senior-level executives in terms of achieving compensation when the firm succeeds, it will reduce dissension and rebellion within the ranks. Fourth and finally, it is important for executives like the CEO to communicate directly with the employees on a regular basis to promote the notion that they appreciate the contributions of the workers.

Companies can also directly incorporate ethics concerns into compensation structures and plans by making ethical performance a metric for compensation. Executives should be aware that they are being judged directly not only on the bottom line, but also on how they reached the bottom line.

As noted above, in order to respond appropriately to regulatory requirements whether already in place or newly enacted pursuant to the Dodd-Frank Act, companies should develop effective and well-thought-out policies and procedures, ensure accountability within the organization, and establish an ethical culture throughout the organization.

2.3 CREATING EFFECTIVE POLICIES AND PROCEDURES

Creating effective policies and procedures is crucial to ensuring that a company is conforming to regulatory requirements and maintaining an ethical culture. These policies and procedures must be carefully crafted so that they meet the needs and goals of the company. First and foremost, policies and procedures should be clear and consistent and easily understood. One should avoid jargon as well as unnecessary and complex wording. The policies and procedures should be written for the employee, not for legal counsel. Policies should also be generally written in a positive manner, rather than focusing on prohibitions or what employees cannot do.

Initially, one should review current and past policies to determine how effective they are or whether they cause confusion or uncertainty. In addition, before even drafting the policies and procedures, one should first clarify the objectives of the particular policy and identify what it is trying to achieve. One should think about why the policy is important before preparing it. It is often helpful to draft an overarching framework policy that sets forth the overall philosophy of the matter at issue as well as specific procedures for undertaking certain tasks. In preparing policies and procedures, one should keep in mind twin goals: (a) setting forth larger strategic objectives, and

(b) providing specificity so that employees know what to do in a particular situation.

Careful attention should be paid to make sure that policies are consistent with each other. If policies are inconsistent in any way, employees will view them as illegitimate and simply ignore them. While remaining consistent, one should also build flexibility into policies and procedures, and allow for exceptions as appropriate. There also must be an easily understood mechanism for amending policies that allows for them to change over time. The process of modifying or amending policies should not be too bureaucratic, or employees will view the process as more trouble than it is worth and choose to disregard them as being outdated.

When finalizing policies and procedures, it is important to obtain "buy-in" from both senior management and employees. Both sets of groups need to have the opportunity to carefully review and comment on the draft policies and procedures and provide feedback for their improvement.

Finally, it is critical for employees to have continuing access to the policies and procedures. It is insufficient to simply have employees sign a piece of paper that they have read the policies and procedures. Employees must be in a position to access them on an ongoing basis. I have had occasion to test companies' policies and procedures in the course of my role as serving as an independent compliance consultant often arising out of SEC and CFTC Enforcement actions with the federal or state government. In the course of my review, I have seen more than one occasion where the policies and procedures were written in a clear and effective manner, but employees were simply not using these policies and procedures in the course of performing their duties at the company. The employees were generally aware of the policies and procedures and recognized that they had reviewed them at one point; however, they were not continuously referring to them in the course of their normal duties.[14] In this scenario, the policies and procedures were well written but rendered essentially meaningless by their lack of use.

---

[14]Continuous and ongoing training on the part of management can assist in employees becoming more familiar with policies and procedures over time.

2.4 ENSURING ACCOUNTABILITY WITHIN AN ORGANIZATION

Ensuring accountability is also a critical component of establishing and maintaining an ethical culture within an organization. An ethical culture exists within an organization where all levels of personnel support ethical values, and adhere to ethical and legal business practices. This adherence can only take place where ethical behavior is practiced on a daily basis. The first step to establishing an ethical culture based upon accountability is to create a clear code of ethics or mission statement. This code or mission statement should be referenced and modeled often by senior management officials and sessions should be set up for employees to understand how to apply the ethics code or mission statement led by the company's ethics officer. This training should include role-playing exercises for employees to contemplate what decisions are appropriate in real-life situations. It is also advisable to set up an ethics review committee of both supervisory and non-supervisory employees to monitor practices within the firm and take appropriate action when unethical behavior is discovered.

Systems should also be developed to both reward ethical conduct and punish unethical behavior. Companies can create incentives to behave ethically and publicly reward such conduct. Companies can authorize employees to nominate their peers for engaging in ethical behavior and have cash bonuses or other forms of compensation presented to those who are found to have acted in an ethical manner. Workplace ethics can also be incorporated into employee performance appraisals, both for employees and for supervisors.

Most importantly, companies need to hold their employees accountable if they engage in unethical behavior or misconduct. While due process is necessary before disciplinary action is taken, once the facts and circumstances have been determined, supervisors need to be willing to reprimand or even terminate an employee who engages in inappropriate activity. Some managers will recoil from the often difficult and unpleasant task of disciplining employees, and maintain that the employee has learned their lesson without formal punishment. Even if this was the case, the other employees in the management unit will see a lack of punishment and believe they will not be held accountable should they engage in unethical behavior in the future.

Furthermore, employees need to believe that those who are being promoted deserve their promotions. If mediocre or underachieving employees are being rewarded or promoted, the incentives to work harder will be lessened significantly. Even for an employee who had a strong work ethic, if he or she sees their peers being promoted to higher positions or given bonuses without earning them, the employee will soon learn that there is little incentive to continue to work hard.

2.5 RED FLAGS OF AN UNETHICAL CULTURE

In assessing how much progress is being made in establishing an ethical culture, several "red flags" are indications that more work is needed to be done. Companies should be wary of a culture with excessive blaming of others for problems within a unit. If certain priorities or goals are not achieved, it is important that employees own up to their responsibility and not always try to find someone else to blame. In these same situations, managers should be accepting responsibility for their decisions and actions that have resulted from their decisions. If the managers are not accepting responsibility, a message will be sent to the employees that they do not need to hold themselves accountable either. In addition, an organization where managers are prone to exaggerating their accomplishments or unrealistically promising rewards to employees can be a sign of a weak ethical culture. Managers should be counseled to be precise with their language and not be viewed as those who make unreliable statements and promises. In addition, while some competition between organizational units may be favorable to productivity, if too many examples of "turf battles" or unnecessary disputes between groups exist, the organization runs the risk of establishing the wrong culture.

2.6 ETHICAL DECISION-MAKING

It may also be worthwhile to consider the concept of "ethical decision-making" and how important decisions at companies are being made. When making a significant decision, one should always think about whether this decision could be damaging to someone or some group. Further, after understanding all the relevant facts, one could evaluate the options through the following different approaches, including which option: (a) produces the most good and least harm; (b) treats people fairly or proportionately; and (c) better serves the community as a whole. Once the decision is made, one should test the decision to see how it turned out, what can be learned from the consequences of that decision, and how it was made.

These approaches can also be incorporated into employee training. As part of substantive training on particular subjects, companies can include a discussion of how ethics factor into what employees do at work on a daily basis. Employees can be reminded to ask themselves the following three questions at the end of each day: (1) Did I do more good than harm today? (2) Did I treat people with dignity and respect today? (3) Did I act in a fair and just manner today? Merely contemplating these questions will lead to employees acting in a more ethical manner in the workplace.

Early in my professional career, while working as an ethics attorney at the U.S. Agency for International Development ("USAID") (the federal Agency that provides foreign aid assistance to countries all over the world), I traveled to many different countries giving "ethical decision-making" seminars to both USAID Foreign Service officers and local nationals. The essence of the seminars was to ask the audience about which values were important to them and how those values impacted their decisions. At each seminar, I asked the group assembled to name different people they admired, their so-called heroes. At every session, as one would expect, different people were named. Often local officials would identify individuals who were important in their native lands. These would generally not be people with whom I was familiar. Next, I asked the audience to identify the particular qualities or characteristics of the individuals named as heroes that they admired. We would compile a long list of these admirable qualities. We then took the long list and narrowed it down to the most important qualities, taking out the ones that were not really values, but behavior. I asked the audience to consider what values they would want a person to use in interacting with their loved ones. We would then go about narrowing the list and invariably, no matter what country we were in, and regardless of the background of the individuals participating in the seminar, the group always coalesced around the same three or four basic values that were agreed upon by all.[15] The seminar taught me that, notwithstanding our differences, we all essentially share the same notions of fairness and compassion and once we realize this fact, it is easier to incorporate these values into our work lives.

During these seminars, I would always cite an example of a company that really understood how to act in an ethical manner. The most common example I gave was that of Johnson & Johnson, and their reaction to a Tylenol scare that occurred many years ago. In the story, a single truck driver was doing his regular route of bringing Tylenol bottles to the drug stores, when he heard a report on his car radio that some of the bottles had been tampered with. I asked the audience to consider what they would do in that situation. This particular driver did not call his supervisor, did not ask any questions, but immediately stopped delivering the bottles and went back to every delivery he had made that day and took all the Tylenol bottles off the shelves. At the same time, as the story goes, hundreds of miles away there was a female Distribution supervisor who worked in a different region and also heard the reports of possible problems with the Tylenol bottles. She also did not call her supervisor, but immediately ordered all Tylenol bottles taken off the shelves in every store in her region. Also at the same time, senior-level management had heard the reports and the FBI came in to meet with them. The FBI told him they were monitoring the developments and had traced the area in which the tampering had taken place to a plant in Tennessee, and by using forensic evidence, they were very close to catching the perpetrator. The FBI asked Johnson & Johnson management not to take

---

[15]These basic values that were identified generally included some variation of compassion, fairness, and loyalty.

any action for 72 hours, as it might compromise their efforts to locate the individual who tampered with the bottles. In the story, Johnson & Johnson management essentially ignored the FBI's instructions, did not check with their Board of Directors, and immediately sent out a press release informing all potential customers of the Tylenol scare and ordering all bottles taken off the shelves. All three individuals were interviewed later and asked what led them to the decision they made. The truck driver was asked why he did not check with anybody before he started pulling the bottles off the shelves. The distribution supervisor was asked why she took the action she did, and management was asked why they did not listen to the FBI. All of them gave essentially the same answer: At Johnson & Johnson, "customer safety comes first." The decisions were easy ones. The Johnson & Johnson credo about the importance of customer safety had been so ingrained into their brains that the decision was automatic. While the Johnson & Johnson story may be more lore than reality, the message was that if one instills into a company's fabric the importance of ethics, making ethical decisions will be easy for all to do.

While it takes time, effort, and resources to instill practices within an organization to establish an ethical culture, organizations are greatly rewarded by emphasizing ethics. A strong ethical culture within a company will help the organization safeguard its assets. Employees will respect the firm's property and keep a careful watch on the bottom line. They will also feel pride in their organizations and will be vigilant to make sure that company resources are not misused. An ethical culture also promotes teamwork and positive motivation among employees. Employees who believe in the company's values will also be harder-working and more productive. Furthermore, companies with reputations as having positive ethical cultures will benefit in recruiting and in retaining workers. Customers also will be more likely to develop trust in this type of organization. The result is more productive, successful, and prosperous organizations.

CHAPTER 3

How to Manage Whistleblowers' Complaints

Whistleblower claims can be a unique challenge for a company. When I served as Inspector General of the SEC between 2007 and 2012, my office received new whistleblower complaints nearly every day. Many of the complaints provided very important information that led to investigations and audits that uncovered significant waste, fraud, and abuse with the SEC's divisions and offices. However, many of these complaints were either nonsensical or contained information that later turned out to be wholly inaccurate. We also received quite a number of complaints from employees facing disciplinary action or termination who were attempting to leverage their complaints in order to make it more difficult for their supervisors to finalize disciplinary action against them. This strategy actually worked in many cases as supervisors were afraid of being accused of retaliation and backed off from disciplinary actions against the whistleblowers when they were informed that a complaint had been filed. This same set of circumstances can, and frequently does, occur in companies who face whistleblower complaints.

3.1 OVERSIGHT AND FAILURES OF THE SEC'S WHISTLEBLOWER PROGRAM

In addition, whistleblower complaints seem to be increasing in recent years, particularly those filed with the SEC as a result of the SEC's recently expanded whistleblower program following the Dodd-Frank Act. Congress mandated that the SEC completely restructure its whistleblower program at least, in part because of a report that I wrote while I served as Inspector General of the SEC. In early 2010, my office conducted an audit of the SEC's whistleblower program. Whistleblower issues and how the SEC managed its whistleblower program were a significant concern on the part of the Congress and the investing public during that period of time, primarily because of the findings that my office had made in connection with an investigation in August 2009 regarding why the SEC failed to uncover Bernie Madoff's $50-billion Ponzi scheme.[1] In this investigation, we found that the SEC ignored and failed to appropriately follow-up on several tips and complaints from whistleblowers that Bernie Madoff was operating a massive Ponzi scheme. Specifically, we found that the SEC had received several detailed and substantive complaints over the years from whistleblowers that should have led them to uncover the Madoff fraud. We found that between June 1992 and December 2008 when Madoff confessed, the SEC received six substantive complaints that raised significant red flags concerning Madoff's hedge fund operations and should have led to questions about whether Madoff was actually engaged in trading.

Our investigation found that the SEC received three versions of a complaint from whistleblower, Harry Markopolos, entitled, "The World's Largest Hedge Fund is a Fraud," which detailed approximately 30 red flags indicating that Madoff was operating a Ponzi scheme, a scenario Markopolos described as "highly likely." Yet, the SEC failed to follow up sufficiently on the red flags identified by Markopolos and never really attempted to verify whether Madoff was perpetrating a Ponzi scheme. In addition, our investigation revealed that SEC personnel were generally skeptical of whistleblowers and whistleblower complaints. We found that an SEC Enforcement attorney, Meaghan Cheung, was skeptical of the Markopolos complaint because she did not believe Markopolos fit the definition of a

---

[1]See *Investigation of the SEC to Uncover Bernard Madoff's Ponzi Scheme*, SEC Office of Inspector General, Report No. OIG-509, August 31, 2009 at http://www.sec.gov/news/studies/2009/oig-509.pdf.

whistleblower since he did not have inside information. In addition, an examiner in the SEC's Office of Compliance Inspections and Examinations, named William Ostrow, stated in our investigation that he did not focus on e-mails he received containing concerns about Madoff's trading, because he generally viewed tips skeptically. In addition, after an anonymous complaint from a whistleblower indicating that there was a "scandal of major proportion" in Madoff's operations was ignored, another SEC Enforcement attorney, Simona Suh, stated that she dismissed the tip without any investigation because in her view anonymous tips "on [their] face" were not credible.

In light of the outrage regarding the SEC's failure to uncover the Madoff fraud and the record of its treatment of whistleblowers, my office, the Office of Inspector General, was requested to scrutinize the SEC's whistleblower program and conducted an audit of that program in early 2010. In the audit, we found that although the SEC has had a bounty program in place for more than 20 years to reward whistleblowers for insider trading tips and complaints, there have been very few payments made to whistleblowers under this program. In addition, the SEC had not even received a large number of applications from individuals seeking a bounty over this 20-year period. Further the audit found that the whistleblower program was not widely known either inside or outside the SEC. Overall, the audit concluded that the SEC whistleblower program was not fundamentally well designed to be successful. We found that the bounty application process was not user-friendly and the criteria for judging bounty applications were broad. In addition, the SEC had not put in place internal policies and procedures to assist staff in assessing contributions made by whistleblowers and making bounty award determinations. In fact, the audit found that the SEC did not provide status reports to whistleblowers regarding their bounty applications, even if a whistleblower's information led to an investigation. Moreover, we found that once bounty applications were received by the SEC and forwarded to appropriate staff for review and further consideration, they were not tracked to ensure they were timely and adequately reviewed. Lastly, the audit found that files regarding bounty referrals did not always contain complete documentation, such as a copy of the bounty application, a memorandum sent to the whistleblower to acknowledge receipt of the application, and a referral memorandum showing the office or division and official to whom the bounty application was referred for further consideration.[2]

As a result of my office's audit findings, we made the following recommendation to the SEC to improve their whistleblower program:

- Develop a communication plan to address outreach to both the public and SEC personnel regarding the SEC whistleblower program. The plan should include efforts to make information available on the SEC's intranet, enhance information available on the SEC's public website, and provide training to employees who are most likely to deal with whistleblower complaints.
- Develop and post to its public website an application form that asks the whistleblower to provide information, including, for example: (a) the facts pertinent to the alleged securities law violation and explanation as to why the whistleblower believes the subject(s) violated the securities laws; (b) a list of related supporting documentation in the whistleblower's possession and available from other sources; (c) a description of how the whistleblower learned about or obtained the information that supports the claim, including the whistleblower's relationship to the subject(s); (d) the amount of any monetary rewards obtained by the subject violator(s) (if known) as a result of the securities law violation, and how the amount was calculated; and (e) a certification that the application is true, correct, and complete to the best of the whistleblower's knowledge.
- Establish policies on when to follow up with whistleblowers who submit applications to clarify information in their applications and obtain readily available supporting documentation prior to making a decision as to whether a whistleblower's complaint should be further investigated.
- Develop specific criteria for recommending the granting of awards, including a provision that where a whistleblower relies

---

[2] See *Assessment of the SEC's Bounty Program*, SEC Office of Inspector General, Report No. 474, March 29, 2010, at http://www.sec.gov/about/offices/oig/reports/audits/2010/474.pdf.

partially upon public information, such reliance will not preclude the individual from receiving an award.

- Examine ways in which the SEC could increase communications with whistleblowers by notifying them of the status of their requests without releasing non-public or confidential information during the course of an investigation or examination.

- Develop a plan to incorporate controls for tracking tips and complaints from whistleblowers seeking awards into the development of Enforcement's tips, complaints, and referrals processes and systems.

- Require that a whistleblower file (hard copy or electronic) be created for each application. The file should contain at a minimum the application, any correspondence with the whistleblower, documentation of how the whistleblower's information was utilized, and documentation regarding significant decisions made with regard to the whistleblower's complaint.

- Incorporate best practices obtained from other whistleblower programs such as the DOJ and Internal Revenue Service ("IRS") programs into the SEC whistleblower program with respect to bounty applications, analysis of whistleblower information, tracking of whistleblower complaints, recordkeeping practices, and continual assessment of the whistleblower program.

- Establish a time frame to finalize new policies and procedures for the SEC whistleblower program that incorporates the best practices from the DOJ and IRS as well as any legislative changes to the program.[3]

3.2 THE DODD-FRANK ACT'S RESTRUCTURING OF THE SEC'S WHISTLEBLOWER PROGRAM

We forwarded our audit findings to Congressional officials and Congress went a step further as part of the Dodd-Frank Act. The Dodd-Frank Act mandated that the SEC adopt a whistleblower program with certain requirements. Specifically, section 922 of the Dodd

---

[3] See ibid.

Frank Act provided that the SEC shall pay awards to eligible whistle-blowers who voluntarily provide the SEC with original information that leads to a successful enforcement action yielding monetary sanctions of over $1 million. The award amount was required to be between 10 percent and 30 percent of the total monetary sanctions collected in the SEC's action or any related action such as in a criminal case. A whistleblower would be eligible to receive an award for original information provided to the Commission on or after July 22, 2010, but before the whistleblower rules become effective, so long as the whistleblower complied with all such rules once effective. The Dodd-Frank Act also expressly prohibited retaliation by employers against whistleblowers and provided them with a private cause of action in the event that they are discharged or discriminated against by their employers in violation of the statute.[4]

On May 25, 2011, the SEC adopted rules to implement the new whistleblower program. The SEC prescribed that to obtain the benefits of the whistleblower award system, a whistleblower must provide "original information," not known to the SEC. This knowledge must originate from the whistleblower's own information or analysis, and not be "exclusively derived" from an allegation made in an official hearing, government report, hearing, audit or investigation, or news media. In addition the whistleblower must be an individual person. A company or other entity would not be eligible to be a whistle-blower. In addition, certain categories of individuals were excluded from receiving monetary awards as a whistleblower, such as officers, directors, trustees, or partners who receive information about a company's alleged violations from a company employee or from the company's internal compliance processes as well as attorneys, compliance personnel, accountants, investigators, and auditors who receive information in the context of a legal representation or in performing compliance or audit duties or a legal investigation, with a few exceptions to this rule.[5]

---

[4]See section 922 of Pub. L. No. 111-203 (July 21, 2010).
[5]See http://www.sec.gov/rules/final/2011/34-64545.pdf. The theory was that insiders such as those identified should not be able to profit through filing whistleblower complaints from information they obtained as part of their duties.

Under the SEC rules, while there is no mandatory requirement for a whistleblower to report internally, significant incentives have been put in place to encourage whistleblowers to report the fraud to their internal compliance offices. For example, a whistleblower may be entitled to an increased award as a direct result of their participation in internal reporting. If a company did not perform an investigation within 120 days and did not report to the SEC within 120 days and the whistleblower does, the whistleblower can receive retroactive credit back to the original date of internal reporting, resulting in significant monetary value to the whistleblower. In essence, the SEC Whistleblower rules effectively created a 120-day window for companies to address internal whistleblower claims.

3.3 WHISTLEBLOWER COMPLAINTS TO THE SEC SINCE THE RESTRUCTURING OF ITS PROGRAM

According to the SEC, in Fiscal Year 2014, they received 3,620 whistleblower complaints.[6] By comparison, the SEC received 3,238 whistleblower complaints in Fiscal Year 2013[7] and 3,001 in Fiscal Year 2012.[8] The most common complaint categories reported by whistleblowers in 2014 were:

- Corporate disclosures and financials (16.9%).
- Offering fraud (16%).
- Manipulation (15.5%).[9]

---

[6]See *2014 Annual Report to Congress on the Dodd-Frank Whistleblower Program,* SEC Office of the Whistleblower at http://www.sec.gov/about/offices/owb/annual-report-2014.pdf. While the SEC does receive a certain percentage of whistleblower complaints that turn out to be unfounded, SEC officials have stated that they have been, for the most part, impressed with the quality of complaints they have received to date.

[7]See *2013 Annual Report to Congress on the Dodd-Frank Whistleblower Program,* SEC Office of the Whistleblower at http://www.sec.gov/about/offices/owb/annual-report-2013.pdf.

[8]See *2012 Annual Report on the Dodd-Frank Whistleblower Program,* SEC Office of the Whistleblower at http://www.sec.gov/about/offices/owb/annual-report-2012.pdf.

[9]See *2014 Annual Report to Congress on the Dodd-Frank Whistleblower Program,* SEC Office of the Whistleblower at http://www.sec.gov/about/offices/owb/annual-report-2014.pdf.

The SEC found similar percentages for complaint categories in both 2013 and 2012:

2013
- Corporate disclosures and financials (17.2%).
- Offering fraud (17.1%).
- Manipulation (16.2%).[10]

2012
- Corporate disclosures and financials (18.2%).
- Offering fraud (15.5%).
- Manipulation (15.2%).[11]

Since the inception of the SEC's whistleblower program in August 2011, the SEC has given out whistleblower awards to 14 whistleblowers, with nine whistleblower awards given in Fiscal Year 2014. The following are some highlights of the awards given:

- August 21, 2012 – The SEC gave its first award to a whistleblower who provided documents and other significant information that allowed an SEC investigation to move at an accelerated pace and prevent the fraud from ensnaring additional victims.[12]
- June 12, 2013 – The SEC issued an award to three whistleblowers who helped it shut down a sham hedge fund. Two of the whistleblowers provided information that prompted the SEC to open the investigation and stop the scheme before more investors were harmed. The third whistleblower provided independent corroborating information and identified key witnesses.[13]
- October 1, 2013 – The SEC announced it had made the largest whistleblower award to date, awarding over $14 million to a whistleblower whose information led to an SEC enforcement

---

[10] See *2013 Annual Report to Congress on the Dodd-Frank Whistleblower Program*, SEC Office of the Whistleblower at http://www.sec.gov/about/offices/owb/annual-report-2013.pdf.

[11] See *2012 Annual Report on the Dodd-Frank Whistleblower Program*, SEC Office of the Whistleblower at http://www.sec.gov/about/offices/owb/annual-report-2012.pdf.

[12] See http://www.sec.gov/News/PressRelease/Detail/PressRelease/1365171483972#.VMak9NhOW70.

[13] See http://www.sec.gov/news/press/2013/2013-06-announcement.htm.

action that recovered substantial investor funds. Less than six months after receiving the whistleblower's tip, the SEC was able to bring an enforcement action against the perpetrators and secure investor funds.[14]

- July 31, 2014 – The SEC announced that it gave more than $400,000 for a whistleblower who reported a fraud to the SEC after the company failed to address the issue internally.[15]
- August 29, 2014 – The SEC stated it gave a whistleblower award of more than $300,000 to an internal auditor who reported corporate wrongdoing to people within the company, including a supervisor. When the company failed to take action within 120 days, the auditor reported the same information to the SEC. It was the first award for a whistleblower with an audit or compliance function at a company.[16]
- September 22, 2014 – The SEC announced its largest award to date, more than $30 million to a whistleblower who provided key original information that led to a successful SEC enforcement action.[17]

3.4   THE CFTC'S NEW WHISTLEBLOWER PROGRAM

The Dodd-Frank Act also created a new whistleblower program at the CFTC, which allows for the payment of monetary awards to eligible whistleblowers, and provides anti-retaliation protection for whistleblowers who share information or assist the CFTC. Section 748 of the Dodd-Frank Act amended the CEA, by adding section 23, entitled "Commodity Whistleblower Incentives and Protection" that established a whistleblower program under which the CFTC

---

[14] See http://www.sec.gov/News/PressRelease/Detail/PressRelease/1370539854258#.VMa ILNhOW70.

[15] See http://www.sec.gov/News/PressRelease/Detail/PressRelease/1370542578457#.VMa IUNhOW70.

[16] See http://www.sec.gov/News/PressRelease/Detail/PressRelease/1370542799812#.VMa mEthOW70.

[17] See http://www.sec.gov/News/PressRelease/Detail/PressRelease/1370543011290#.VMa l6thOW70.

would pay awards to eligible whistleblowers who voluntarily provide the Commission with original information about violations of the CEA that lead either to a "covered judicial or administrative action" or a "related action."[18] CEA section 23 also established the Commodity Futures Trading Commission Customer Protection Fund (the "Fund"), which is used to pay whistleblower awards and to fund customer education initiatives designed to help customers protect themselves against fraud or other violations.[19] Similar to the new SEC whistleblower program, the CFTC pays awards where the information leads to an Enforcement action that results in more than $1 million in monetary sanctions; the total amount of a whistleblower award will be between 10 percent and 30 percent of the monetary sanctions collected.[20] In addition, as with the SEC rules, a 120-day period is set as the time frame in which the expectation is that the company will have conducted the investigation.[21]

The CFTC had paid one award as of February 2015 and in Fiscal Year 2014, received 227 whistleblower tips and complaints.[22] The award announced by the CFTC on May 20, 2014 was to an individual in the amount of $240,000 for providing valuable information about violations of the CEA.[23]

3.5   SIGNIFICANT U.S. SUPREME COURT DECISION ON WHISTLEBLOWER COMPLAINTS

With each new award given to whistleblowers, the incentives to file claims increase. In addition, a March 2014 U.S. Supreme Court case ruled that whistleblower protections should be extended to employees of contractors of public companies, in a decision that will likely significantly increase the number of whistleblower complaints filed.

---

[18] See section 748 of Pub. L. No. 111-203 (July 21, 2010).

[19] See ibid.

[20] See http://www.cftc.gov/ConsumerProtection/WhistleblowerProgram/index.htm.

[21] See CFTC Whistleblower Rules at http://www.cftc.gov/ucm/groups/public/@whistleblowernotices/documents/file/whistleblowerrules17cfr165.pdf.

[22] See *2014 Annual Report on the Whistleblower Program and Customer Education Initiatives*, CFTC at http://www.cftc.gov/ucm/groups/public/@whistleblowernotices/documents/file/wb_fy2014reporttocongress.pdf.

[23] See http://www.cftc.gov/PressRoom/PressReleases/pr6933-14.

In the case, *Lawson v. FMR*, a former senior director of finance at a mutual fund claimed she was retaliated against for disclosing certain cost-accounting improprieties. The lower court ruled that the anti-retaliation law only applies to employees of public companies, and as the mutual fund in this case operated its funds with zero employees under a contracting arrangement with separately incorporated investment advisers, the whistleblower was not entitled to protection. The Supreme Court, in a decision by Justice Ruth Bader Ginsburg, rejected the argument that only direct employees of public companies should receive protection and expanded the coverage of an anti-retaliation claim under the Sarbanes-Oxley Act of 2002 ("SOX") to employees of a privately-held contractor.[24] The effect will be that many more individuals will have the right to file suit claiming retaliation and will be more incentivized to bring whistleblower claims.

3.6 MANAGING COMPLAINTS BROUGHT TO INTERNAL COMPLIANCE OFFICIALS

The SEC is also reporting that, in all but a handful of cases, whistleblowers are bringing their claims first to the company's internal compliance officials. This choice is positive news for internal compliance officials at firms as they have the ability to manage the whistleblower claims within the 120-day window that has been established in the SEC whistleblower rules. Accordingly, it is critical for companies to act within the first 120 days from which they receive the whistleblower complaint. If companies are able to conduct investigations within that time frame, they will be in a position to limit their exposure as by the time the matter is brought to the regulators' attention, the company is able to demonstrate that they have taken appropriate action and are much more knowledgeable about their vulnerabilities, having had the benefit of the complete investigation. Investigations conducted within 120 days will also limit the type of employees who can bring whistleblower complaints to the SEC. As referenced above,

---

[24]See full decision in matter entitled, *Lawson v. FMR LLC*, 571 U.S. ___ (2014) at https://supreme.justia.com/cases/federal/us/571/12-3/opinion3.html.

in September 2014, the SEC announced it was granting an internal auditor a whistleblower award of more than $300,000. The internal auditor had reported corporate wrongdoing to individuals with the company, including a supervisor. However, when the company took no action on the information within 120 days, the whistleblower reported the same information to the SEC. The information provided by the internal auditor whistleblower led to an SEC Enforcement action. The chief of the SEC's whistleblower office said that "individuals who perform internal audit, compliance, and legal functions for companies" may be eligible for an SEC whistleblower award "if their companies fail to take appropriate, timely action on information they first reported internally." Conducting investigations of whistleblowing complaints within the 120-day period will ensure that internal auditors and others who have access to information due to their auditing and compliance roles will keep the information in-house rather than reporting it to the government.

Conducting a swift and comprehensive investigation of whistleblowing allegations will also enable the company to make an educated judgment on what actions they should take next. If the investigation finds that the whistleblower complaint did not have merit, the company should ensure that they obtain a complete and comprehensive report of investigation that they can show the government if the matter escalates. As a result of limited resources – which is the case for government Agencies like the SEC and CFTC – if a complaint is brought to their attention against a company, and that company can show that the allegations were investigated thoroughly by a credible party, they will likely choose not to investigate the matter further. In addition, in a situation where the investigation finds that the whistleblower complaint lacked merit, and at the same time, the employee who brought the complaint was facing disciplinary action or termination, the company will be in a stronger legal position to take action against the employee if it can show that it dealt credibly with the employee's whistleblower complaint, and any action it takes against the employee is not retaliatory, but related to completely separate issues concerning the employee's performance or misconduct. However, any decision on disciplinary or administrative actions against an employee who has brought a whistleblower complaint must be made with the assistance of counsel, particularly if the complaint has been brought to the attention of the government. The SEC or CFTC, for example, could determine that although the underlying complaint brought by the whistleblower is without an evidentiary basis, it nevertheless may take action against a company for retaliation against the employee if an employee is disciplined or terminated within a short time frame after the employee brought the whistleblower complaint.

Should the investigation conducted within the 120-day period find that the whistleblower complaint does have merit, the company has a decision to make, regarding whether they should self-report the information to a governmental Agency, and also must determine whether they are required to modify their financial statements or otherwise make a filing or submission as a result of the findings in the investigation. Certainly, if the investigation disclosed something that would require a modification of financial statements or other required filing by the company, the disclosure must be made as soon as possible. In addition, if the firm knows that the whistleblower intends to report the matter to the regulator, and the allegations raised by the whistleblower have some merit, it is a good idea for the firm to communicate with the regulator so that the regulator is aware that the matter has been investigated and the company plans to take appropriate remedial measures.

In other situations, the decision of whether to self-report to the regulator must be made based upon the specific facts known at the time. Generally, the greater the wrongdoing, the greater the reason that exists to report the matter to the regulator. If the investigation disclosed, for example, widespread fraud within the company or an egregious action by a senior-level official within the company, such as embezzlement, disclosure should be made. In this scenario, it may be important from a public relations perspective for the company to "get ahead of the message." If the investigation disclosed a minor problem that can be remedied relatively easily, it may make sense not to self-report unless there is a legal obligation to do so. While the SEC has indicated that it will reward cooperation and self-reporting, the costs of an investigation on a company may be high, and if the problem can be fixed internally, it may not make sense from a cost–benefit perspective to disclose what occurred to the government.

Whether the company intends to self-report to the government or not, it remains critical that it conduct a thorough and credible investigation within the 120-day window. In addition, while a company's first instinct may be to have in-house counsel, or an in-house investigative group, conduct the investigation, for allegations that look to be serious, it may make more sense to retain an outside investigator. Even the company's law firm, if that firm has represented the company for many years, may not be the best choice because it will seem as if the investigation is not being conducted by an impartial entity. Having an outside firm with no prior ties to the company will substantially bolster the credibility of the investigation in the eyes of the SEC, CFTC, or the DOJ. I have seen situations where the government rejected completely an investigative report that was conducted by a long-time counsel for a company regardless of how thorough it was, because they felt the investigation was not conducted by an unbiased source.

The investigation must be conducted in a thorough and comprehensive manner and conclude with a full report of investigation. It is critical that the report of investigation be well-written and persuasive. The report should also include specific and concrete recommendations that the company is able to implement within a reasonable time frame after the investigation is concluded. The company should be prepared to deal with the findings and to demonstrate how they have learned from the incident and modified their policies, procedures, and operations accordingly.[25]

It is also important to keep ongoing communications with the whistleblower (assuming the whistleblower is not anonymous) during the investigation process if at all possible. The company should keep the whistleblower generally appraised of the status of the investigation, although substantive information about the investigation cannot be shared until it is concluded. If the company decides to self-report to the government, it should inform the whistleblower that it has taken this action. The company should also advise the whistleblower of remedial measures that it plans to take, as a result

---

[25]For a more detailed discussion of internal investigation, see Chapter 13, entitled, "How to Conduct Internal Investigations."

of the investigation's findings. Whistleblowers will be more likely to go to the government if they believe that their complaint is not being taken seriously, or if they feel nothing is being done to change the operations of the company as a result of their complaint. Keeping them in the loop on the impact of their complaint and the resulting investigation will go a long way to ensuring that they feel like their actions have meaning and they will be less likely to report the information outside of the company.

If a decision is made to report the findings of the investigation to the regulator, one should be prepared to discuss more than just the investigative findings when meeting with the regulator. The regulator will be interested to hear about the company's entire whistleblower program and internal policies and procedures. One should be prepared to discuss the company's compliance and ethics program and how management sets the appropriate "tone at the top." One should describe the hotlines in place and how efforts are made to encourage whistleblowers to come forward. One should also explain the company's process for investigating whistleblower allegations and how it ensures that retaliation does not occur. Finally, one should describe the company's compliance training, including discussions on whistleblowing.

3.7 PUTTING APPROPRIATE WHISTLEBLOWER POLICIES AND PROCEDURES IN PLACE

Of course, these policies and procedures need to be in place prior to the need to report to the regulator. Companies must have anonymous hotlines or other mechanisms for reporting suspected or actual misconduct confidentially and without fear of retaliation. When an employee submits a complaint through the whistleblower hotline, the information should be immediately distributed and the employee should be informed that the information he or she provided has been received. In a small company, the hotline may direct all complaints to the attention of one designated person at the company. That person can then promptly address the complaints and inform the audit committee of any material issues. Larger organizations often hire outside contractors to receive complaints. Outside contractors can be very useful in providing employees with assurances about anonymity and confidentiality, can handle complaints 24 hours a day, seven days a week, and offer a wide range of ways to communicate their complaints, such as e-mail, web forms, or telephone hotlines. In these larger companies, the complaints are generally sent to a committee or team for review and to make sure the more serious complaints are forwarded to the audit committee.

Employees must also be trained to understand the whistleblower hotline program and the process. Board members and management officials should also undergo this training. In addition, the company should maintain a confidential recordkeeping system that will enable it to review the subsequent employment history of employees who have made whistleblowing complaints so that it can document that it has treated those employees favorably and not engaged in any retaliation.

Finally, every employee should be provided a link to a written procedure for filing a complaint. The company's policies should include a non-retaliation statement that encourages employees to come forward with complaints of unlawful conduct without fear of retaliation. Management officials and supervisors should also be trained on what constitutes retaliation.

Having these policies and procedures in place will assist the company greatly if it decides that it has to self-report to the regulator. The company will be able to demonstrate that its culture encourages whistleblowers and treats their complaints appropriately in the specific case it is raising and in general. Companies may also be able point to their favorable treatment of whistleblowers and policies against retaliation.

3.8 EFFECT OF THE SEC AND CFTC'S NEW WHISTLEBLOWER PROGRAMS

Overall, the impact of the SEC and CFTC's new whistleblower program is significant. As incentives increase even further with more whistleblower awards, more whistleblowers will be encouraged to come forward, and companies will have to adapt by conducting extensive internal investigations prior to the SEC or CFTC conducting its own investigation, and by putting into place policies and procedures to ensure that they are able to convince the government that they have a corporate culture that incentivizes both positive and negative feedback within the company. The SEC has changed considerably since it failed to take the whistleblower complaints about Bernie Madoff seriously. The new SEC whistleblower program creates incentives within the SEC to encourage and listen to whistleblowers. Companies need to do the same. By conducting credible and thorough investigations within the 120-day time frame, companies can limit their liability and exposure and by communicating with whistleblowers through the process, companies can convince these employees that they are being responsible with the information provided to them, and that there is no need for the matter to be escalated outside of the company.

CHAPTER 4

How to Defend SEC Examinations

The regulatory Agencies and SROs conduct periodic and cause examinations of firms under their jurisdiction to inspect their records and ensure that the firms are complying with all applicable rules and regulations. The examination process can last for several weeks or even longer both on and off-site and can be extremely stressful for firms that are also attempting to continue to operate their substantive businesses while the examinations are ongoing. The next three chapters provide firms with practical, hands-on advice for defending the different types of examinations commenced by the SEC, FINRA, and NFA.

4.1 SEC AUTHORITY TO CONDUCT EXAMINATIONS

Under section 17 of the Securities Exchange Act of 1934, the SEC has authority to conduct inspections over registered broker-dealers. Section 17(b) of the Exchange Act states that "[a]ll records of [defined to include broker-dealers] ... are subject at any time, or from time to time, to such reasonable periodic, special, or other examinations by representatives of the [SEC] and the appropriate regulatory agency for such persons as the [SEC] or the appropriate regulatory agency for such persons deems necessary or appropriate in the public interest, for the protection of investors ..."[1] Section 17(a) of the Exchange

---

[1] 15 U.S.C. § 78q.

Act states that registered broker-dealers "shall make and keep for prescribed periods such records, furnish such copies thereof, and make and disseminate such reports as the [SEC], by rule, prescribes as necessary or appropriate in the public interest, for the protection of investors ..."[2]

Section 204 of the Investment Advisers Act of 1940 ("Investment Advisers Act") authorizes the SEC to conduct "at any time, or from time to time ... such reasonable periodic, special, or other examinations [of investment advisers] ... as the [SEC] deems necessary or appropriate in the public interest or for the protection of investors."[3] Rule 204-2 under the Investment Advisers Act requires registered investment advisers to make and keep true, accurate books and records in connection with their investment advisory business.[4] Specifically, registered investment advisers are required to maintain the following books and records: (1) journals, including cash receipts/disbursements, records, and any other records of original entry forming the basis of entries in any ledger; (2) ledgers reflecting assets, liabilities, reserves, capital, and income and expense reports; (3) memoranda of orders given by the investment adviser for the purchase or sale of any security; (4) check books, bank statements, and cash reconciliations; (5) bills or statements relating to the business of the registered investment advisers; (6) trial balances, financial statements, and internal audit working papers relating to the business of the registered investment adviser; (7) originals of written communications received and copies of written communications sent by the registered investment adviser related to recommendations, receipt/disbursements of funds or securities, or placing or executing any order to purchase or sell; and (8) written agreements entered into by the investment adviser with any client or otherwise relating to the business of the investment adviser as such.[5]

---

[2] 15 U.S.C. § 78q(a)(1).
[3] 15 U.S.C. § 80b-4(a).
[4] 17 C.F.R. § 275.204-2(a).
[5] 17 C.F.R. § 275.204-2(a).

4.2 SEC'S OFFICE OF COMPLIANCE INSPECTIONS AND EXAMINATIONS (OCIE)

Examinations of both broker-dealers and investment advisers are conducted by the SEC's OCIE, which is headquartered in Washington, D.C., and has a presence in the SEC's regional offices all across the country. In addition to having exam authority over registered investment advisers and registered broker-dealers, OCIE has responsibility for conducting examinations of investment companies, transfer agents, and SROs.

OCIE's mission is to protect investors, ensure market integrity, and support responsible capital formation through risk-focused strategies that: (1) improve compliance; (2) prevent fraud; (3) monitor risk; and (4) inform policy.[6] The results of OCIE's examinations are utilized by the SEC to inform rule-making initiatives, identify and monitor risks, improve industry practices, and pursue misconduct.[7]

4.3 TYPES OF SEC OCIE EXAMS

The SEC's OCIE conducts various types of examinations. The primary types are routine, cause, and sweep examinations. Routine examinations are generally conducted according to a cyclical schedule based on the firm's business activities and risk profile as determined by OCIE. Cause examinations are generally initiated by OCIE based on information regarding the possibility of wrongdoing or violations at the company. Sweep examinations are initiated by OCIE in order to focus on a particular issue or practice within the industry. OCIE also conducts oversight examinations of registered broker-dealers where they have been recently examined by an SRO, such as FINRA and other risk-based examinations as necessary.

Amy Lynch, a recognized expert on SEC examinations, describes a recent new type of SEC exam, called a presence exam, for newly registered private equity and hedge funds, which is a short form of

---

[6]http://www.sec.gov/ocie/Article/about.html#.VH4HpNhOW70.
[7]Ibid.

an examination where the SEC examiners are on-site for a few days making sure that the firms have certain basic compliance procedures and processes in place.[8] Lynch has over 20 years of experience in the financial industry, beginning her career working for OCIE in both the SEC's New York and Washington, D.C. offices. At the SEC, Lynch was responsible for conducting examinations of mutual funds, investment advisers, and insurance firms nationwide. Lynch has also worked for FINRA Enforcement and is the founder and President of FrontLine Compliance, a full-service independent consulting firm providing regulatory compliance services to investment advisers, broker-dealers, hedge funds, private equity firms, investment companies, and insurance company affiliates.

4.4 PREPARATION FOR THE EXAMS

Lynch explains that firms need to prepare well in advance in order to be ready for a regulatory examination. Preparation is the best line of defense. A firm (called a "registrant" by the regulators) will never know which type of exam it is facing, but there are ways to make the determination. If one is facing a cause exam (an exam brought because of a specific complaint or piece of information brought to the regulator's attention), Lynch advises that firms attempt to initially learn what the SEC is concerned about by seeing what kind of books and records the examiners are seeking from the company. It is important to analyze the document requests as soon as they are provided. Once firms gain this understanding, they can, according to Lynch, attempt to quickly determine the extent of the risks involved and that will inform their next steps. Lynch also points out that firms with strong compliance programs should already be aware of areas with potential exposure, and if they are completely surprised by an area of vulnerability being examined by the SEC, questions should arise about the effectiveness of their internal controls. Lynch also advises that it is worth trying to identify which department

---

[8]These presence exams, based upon an SEC program begun in October 2012, focus on risk-based compliance areas, tailored to the risk profile of the individual firm, as well as areas of SEC regulatory priority.

at the SEC is initiating the exam. She points out that if one has SEC Enforcement staff involved from the beginning of the exam, it could be a troubling sign. However, she notes that the office of asset management within SEC Enforcement does have investigators that work with the examination teams and OCIE, and, therefore the involvement of Enforcement does not necessarily mean the exam will lead to an Enforcement investigation or action. Lynch also explains that sometimes it may be difficult to determine the impetus for the exam as the SEC is unlikely to tell a firm, "This is a cause exam, or this is just a routine exam." It is often up to the firm to try to figure it out themselves.

Where a company is faced with a routine examination, it may have a greater ability to prepare in advance for the examination. In preparation for a routine examination, firms may elect to have a mock examination or audit conducted by a consulting firm to help identify potential deficiencies or challenges in the firm's compliance program. Lynch explains that the term "mock audit" or "mock exam" is widely misused in the industry. A firm can pay $5,000 for a one-day, on-site "mock audit" or $250,000 for an extensive review that takes months; and of course, there are many varieties in-between. The key is to find the type of review that will be most meaningful for the firm given its age, size, asset types, business model, etc. Most importantly, the review should provide value by leaving the firm with a sense of accomplishment and a positive direction for its compliance program, even when faced with the need for corrective measures.

Lynch advises that the mock exam or audit should be conducted by someone who has an understanding of how examinations are conducted by SEC examiners, including obtaining copies of the actual document requests being used by the SEC at that time and the process should take the firm through similar steps faced during a real SEC exam. Lynch explains that a key component of this mock exam is to make sure that the firm's staff, not just the Chief Compliance Officer ("CCO") or the General Counsel ("GC"), but all of the staff, including the head trader, the analysts, the portfolio managers, the CFO, the Chief Operating Officer ("COO"), and the CEO understand what is going to happen in the exam, such as the types of questions that are going to be asked and what each individual's role will be during the exam.

Companies should be aware that results of mock exams will likely be considered an internal audit report that will be available to the SEC during an examination. The tone and substance of the report must keep this in mind. Lynch explains that she also tells her clients who go through the mock audit process that they should expect findings and must be willing to address and remedy the findings so that they are not discovered during an actual SEC exam. Certain measures can also be taken to prepare for the arrival of the SEC examiners. Files regarding prior exams or reviews should be examined before the SEC examiners arrive. These files should be reviewed to ensure that the firm has addressed any issues or deficiencies noted in the prior regulatory exams.

Firms should prepare for the exams by compiling relevant documents that can be useful to show the SEC during the exam. An example of these documents would be compliance records, including evidence of training designed to demonstrate to the examiners that the firm has established a strong culture of compliance. In addition, as often examiners will request to take a tour of the firm's facilities, office space, and trading floor, as appropriate, steps should be taken to ensure that the office space to be viewed is clean and organized, and sensitive information is secured.

4.5   PROCESS OF EXAMINATIONS

Generally, the routine exam process begins when a firm receives a phone call from the lead examiner, followed by an initial letter from the SEC. The letter often seeks general documentation about the firm, such as organizational diagrams, lists of employees, compliance policies and procedures, and financial documents and begins to seek data needed for the exam. The firm should carefully review the letter and provide the requested documents in a timely manner. Lynch advises that a common mistake made by firms facing an SEC examination is that they let their anxiety cause them to overreact. She explains that it is natural to be anxious when one hears the SEC will conduct an audit. However, this may result in firms being too anxious to respond to the SEC. Lynch provides the example of the SEC document request in which the SEC indicates it wishes to see several items before their staff arrive on-site, and that they plan to arrive in three weeks. Lynch advises that there is no reason to rush the response to the SEC. If one provides the documentation and information immediately, Lynch explains that the SEC has two-and-a-half weeks to look at the firm's data before they come on-site. She notes that it is one thing to be responsive and make sure one is producing what is requested, but there is no need to give them extra time to go over the documents and decide what they are going to dig into once they come on-site.

With respect to document requests, Lynch emphasizes how it is important for the firm to carefully track everything they are handing over. Lynch states she has seen instances where firms are so eager to provide responsive documents to the examiners that they start handing over documents without analyzing them internally. Lynch notes that this could be a major problem because one could be handing over something that contains a red flag and not even know it.

It is also important to respond to document requests from examiners in an organized manner. The approach of providing copious amounts of documents in an effort to overwhelm the examiner is not an advisable one. This decision could not only aggravate the examiner, but also unnecessarily prolong the examination. The firm should consider either bates-stamping or providing the examiner with an index of documents provided so that both parties can keep track of the documentation.

One should also ensure that a conference room is reserved and there is adequate space for the examiners to work while they are on-site. While often examiners are given computer terminals to facilitate their work, one should make sure that this does not provide the examiners unfettered access to all of the firm's operating systems.

Often, there is an entrance conference on one of the first days that the examiners arrive at the firm's offices. At this entrance conference, the firm should be prepared to answer questions regarding the firm's organizational structure, business lines, revenue sources, operations, types and nature of clients, and compliance environment, including internal controls and pending regulatory actions. It is often helpful to have someone from senior management attend the entrance conference to emphasize the importance management places on compliance.

Lynch recommends that firms designate a point person, usually the CCO, as the firm contact for the examiners, who would participate in every meeting and facilitate information being provided to the examiners. Lynch advises that the point person check in with the on-site examiners at least once a day to make sure the examiners have what they need and are not wandering around interviewing staff without the CCO present.

In general, the point person and the firm's employees should make sure not to treat the examiners as adversaries, and establish a collegial level of dialogue with them. Meetings with the examiners, even interviews of management should be viewed as opportunities for the firm to explain to the examiners how their business operates, rather than trying to argue their positions to them. The firm should also try to be candid and up-front with the examiners, and not hide behind badly-phrased questions to omit information that is clearly being sought. The point person should return examiners' calls promptly, even if they do not have responsive information. A prompt return call can build goodwill by simply saying that the call was received, and efforts are being made to locate the information or documentation requested.

Normally, Lynch notes that the General Counsel (if any) should attend the entrance meeting or conference if one is scheduled, and the exit conference, but the General Counsel may not necessarily have additional direct contact with the examiners unless a legal issue arises during the course of the examination. Lynch also states that unless there are extenuating circumstances, there is not a need to have outside counsel to the firm participate in the exam process. The SEC tends to view the use of outside counsel during the exam as an attempt to stall or "hide" information. The presence of outside attorneys may lead to the examiners becoming more aggressive and less communicative during the exam which could lead to misunderstandings regarding findings.

Interviews of firm employees routinely occur in SEC examinations. For all interviews, it is important that the point of contact be present. Preparation of the employees being interviewed is also important. The interviewees need to understand the scope of the interview, and the questions that are likely to be asked. Any relevant documents that have been produced to the examiners should be reviewed by the interviewees in-depth prior to the interview. Employees should understand that they need to be able to explain their job duties in the interview and should appreciate that the appropriate tone in the interview should be collegial, rather than adversarial. The interviewee should be instructed not to speculate or guess at answers during the interview, and that it is perfectly appropriate for them to say, "I don't know; that is not my area of responsibility." The firm point of contact should make sure not to disrupt the interview in any way, but can interject to clarify questions, and even make sure that the examiner's questions are limited to the pre-arranged scope of the interview. The point of contact can also suggest a particular employee for a separate interview should it become clear that the current interviewee is answering questions that are not part of his or her purview.

If the point person or CCO believes that the SEC is identifying a serious compliance issue during the course of the exam, one approach is to hire a consultant who has experience with SEC exams to determine the extent of the issue and what actions to take as a result. Lynch notes that consultants can help determine if the CCO's concerns are warranted or not, and advise the firm whether the issue is serious enough to necessitate the retention of outside counsel. Lynch also explains that there have been instances where the SEC examiners simply did not understand the firm's business model and did not understand how various areas interacted with each other within the firm, thinking that there was a compliance or other issue based upon this lack of understanding. In these types of situations, consultants can assist the firm in educating the SEC examiners and avoid an issue altogether.

While it does not occur frequently, there are occasions where firms have to deal with inexperienced and, sometimes, difficult or even combative examiners. Lynch explains that the inexperienced examiner who admits that they have not been at the SEC for very long and are just trying to understand how the firm operates is much easier to deal with because one can try to help the examiner to understand how things actually work at the firm and in the industry. According to Lynch, when a firm faces an examiner that is just the opposite, and is antagonistic, this can be more difficult to handle because it is important for the firm contact to be responsive to even an irrational examiner, but not combative in return. Lynch counsels that there are instances where it is necessary to contact a supervisor, for example, where one has a really combative examiner that simply does not understand something, notwithstanding repeated efforts made to provide an explanation.

Lynch explains that the junior-level SEC examiners on an exam may be only a few years out of college, while the more senior examiner on the team would have at least three to four years of experience working at the SEC. Lynch notes that in recent years and given all the scrutiny of the SEC relating to the financial crisis and their failures to uncover significant frauds like Bernie Madoff's $50 billion Ponzi scheme, even after having conducted several examinations, the SEC has been hiring more experienced people from the industry to join their examination program. In general, Lynch believes this is positive as the examiners are more likely to understand the firms' businesses. On the other hand, Lynch notes that this may also result in SEC examiners digging deeper and finding things faster than before. In addition, according to Lynch, there may be instances where the more experienced examiners begin the exam with certain preconceived potential issues and they are determined to discover those issues at the firm even though they may not exist. On these cases, Lynch counsels that the firm needs to calmly explain to the examiner "Yes, we do it differently. We do not do it the way your previous employer did or the way you have seen it at other firms (which may be of concern to the SEC) but this is how we do it and we think this is correct because of A, B, C, D and we have the documentation to show you." The key, according to Lynch, is to explain that, just because it is different, does not mean a regulatory issue exists. Typically, there are several ways to achieve a compliant outcome.

The exam generally ends with an exit interview where the SEC examiners set forth their preliminary findings. Lynch notes that the exit interview is often the firm's first opportunity to find out what the examiners are thinking. She advises firms to use this meeting to attempt to clarify issues that the SEC has raised, and, if necessary, to provide additional documentation to the examiners that might shed further light on potential SEC findings. Lynch also notes that even after the exit conference, firms have the ability to go back and conduct their own analysis of the issues raised in the interview and provide the examiners with additional information or documentation following the interview that could be helpful to the firm. She also recommends that if the SEC raises an issue at the exit conference that surprises the firm and may result in deficiencies that the firm believes are incorrect, it is advisable to retain a consulting firm to assist the firm in convincing the SEC to change its position. A good consultant can help resolve a misunderstanding between the firm and the examiners by serving as a neutral third party to the issue with the ability to understand the issue from both sides. This is crucial to finding a resolution that satisfies both the SEC and the firm.

4.6   HOW THE SEC EXAM CONCLUDES

The examination may conclude in one of the following three ways: (1) no findings or deficiencies; (2) deficiencies identified in a letter that will require corrective actions; and (3) a referral of the matter to SEC Enforcement for further investigation. Lynch notes that only about 2 percent of all SEC exams conclude with no findings. Deficiency letters can vary considerably in length and scope as well as in the level of seriousness of the issues contained in the letter. Lynch points out that those deficiencies that relate to a lack of internal controls do not bode well for the firm.

If the SEC deficiency letter includes a significant number of deficiencies and includes language to the effect that "this indicates a lack of internal controls," according to Lynch, firms should be worried that the SEC feels there may be some systemic issues that need to be addressed and may wish to return to the firm in the near future to check on the status of these issues. If this does occur, Lynch advises that the firm consider carefully scrutinizing their compliance unit, perhaps with the assistance of an outside consulting firm. In a deficiency letter, the SEC will identify certain deficiencies of the firm and request that the firm provide a written response addressing such issues. In responding to a deficiency letter, firms should make sure to include information describing corrective action taken to address the issues identified by the staff and documentation supporting or memorializing the corrective action. It is important for firms to respond to the particular issue identified in the deficiency letter without providing any unnecessary or irrelevant information.

If a referral is made to SEC Enforcement, outside counsel should be retained. In this case, firms should expect the SEC Enforcement staff to request additional information and conduct testimony of firm employees. If a determination is made to move forward with formal action, the SEC Enforcement staff will likely provide a notice informing the firm of the proposed violations.

4.7   SEC OCIE EXAMINATION TRENDS

Firms should also be aware of several SEC OCIE examination trends. In April 2014, OCIE issued a risk alert ("alert") announcing its plan to conduct examinations to assess cybersecurity preparedness in the securities industry. As part of this initiative, OCIE intended to conduct examinations of more than 50 registered broker-dealers and registered investment advisers focused on: (1) the entity's cybersecurity governance; (2) identification and assessment of cybersecurity risks; (3) protection of networks and information; (4) risks associated with remote customer access and funds transfer requests; (5) risks associated with vendors and other third parties; (6) detection of unauthorized activity, and (7) experiences with certain cybersecurity threats.[9] The purpose of the cybersecurity examinations is to help identify areas where the SEC and the industry can work together to protect investors and our capital markets from cybersecurity threats.

---

[9] See http://www.sec.gov/ocie/announcement/Cybersecurity+Risk+Alert++%2526+Appendix+-+4.15.14.pdf.

In addition, since the Madoff scandal, custody of assets has been a major priority for OCIE with respect to investment advisers and investment companies. In the investigation I conducted of the failure of the SEC to uncover the Madoff Ponzi scheme while I served as Inspector General of the SEC, I found that OCIE conducted numerous cause exams of Madoff's operations based upon specific and detailed tips and complaints that gave the indications that Madoff might be operating a major fraud. Notwithstanding these examinations, at no time did the SEC take the basic step of attempting to verify Madoff's trading through an independent third party. In addition, SEC examiners never took any real steps to verify the custody of the assets and never determined how Madoff executed and cleared trades. As a result of these failures, SEC examinations have included a particular emphasis on advisers who fail to comply with the requirements of the Custody Rule.[10]

4.8 NOT UNDERESTIMATING THE SEC EXAMINERS

As discussed above, another impact of the Madoff scandal is that the SEC has hired more experienced examiners who are better equipped to scrutinize broker-dealers and investment advisers. Of all the examinations to which a firm may be subject, it is likely that the SEC examinations will be led by the most capable and experienced examiners. However, no matter how experienced, these examiners are going to have a difficult time understanding the firm – or even the industry – as well as the firm's own management and many of its employees. Accordingly, the best method of defending SEC examinations is to educate SEC examiners without being antagonistic, or talking down to them. Using this approach and with the proper preparation, as long as the firms can demonstrate a strong culture of compliance, they can get through SEC exams without significant deficiencies and too much aggravation.

---

[10]The Custody Rule, found in Rule 206(4)-2 of the Investment Advisers Act, was promulgated to protect assets managed by registered investment advisers. Under the rule, a registered investment adviser must maintain client funds and securities with a "qualified custodian" in accounts that contain only client funds and must segregate and identify client securities and hold them in a reasonably safe place.

CHAPTER 5

How to Defend FINRA Examinations

FINRA is a private SRO registered with and overseen by the SEC pursuant to certain provisions of the Exchange Act.[1] While FINRA is owned and operated by its members, all of its rules and regulations must be approved by the SEC. FINRA requires registration of any broker-dealers effecting securities transactions by means of interstate commerce.[2] Additionally, in some circumstances, persons who provide services to broker-dealers, such as investment bankers, consultants, intermediaries, and finders, may be required to register as broker-dealers if they engage in activities that are characteristic of brokers or dealers. FINRA also has jurisdiction over the NASDAQ market and the many products traded on the over-the-counter ("OTC") markets. The OTC markets include equities traded in the OTC and on the OTC Bulletin Board, third market trades of securities listed on national exchanges, and government and municipal securities. In addition, FINRA regulates members' activities in corporate debt, mutual funds, direct participation programs, limited

---

[1]The SEC delegates to SROs like FINRA authority to oversee both securities markets and participants in those markets. The SRO can be either in a national exchange, such as the New York Stock Exchange ("NYSE"), or a national securities association like FINRA.

[2]See Securities Exchange Act of 1934, codified at 15 U.S.C. section 78a *et seq.* The determination of what constitutes broker-dealer activity is a matter of fact and includes: (a) participation in the solicitation, negotiation, or execution of securities transactions; (b) receiving transaction-based compensation; or (c) holding investor funds or securities.

partnerships, and variable annuities. FINRA also enforces rules for municipal securities, though the rules are passed by the Municipal Securities Rulemaking Board ("MSRB") and approved by the SEC.

FINRA is the successor entity to the National Association of Securities Dealers (the "NASD"). In 2007, FINRA was formed when the NASD merged with certain regulatory divisions of the New York Stock Exchange.

5.1 FINRA QUALIFICATION STANDARDS AND RULES AND REGULATIONS

FINRA sets forth strict qualification standards that all prospective members must meet prior to becoming FINRA members. Admission requirements of FINRA include:

- Meeting net capital requirements.
- Having at least two principals to supervise the firm.
- Having one year of direct, or two years of related experience, for each person charged with supervision and each principal and registered representative of the firm must take and pass the requisite securities qualification examinations.
- Meeting Anti-Money Laundering ("AML") requirements.
- Meeting audit trail reporting requirements.[3]

FINRA develops rules and regulations, conducts regulatory reviews of members' business activities, and designs and operates marketplace services and facilities. FINRA may request information from its member firms pursuant to its rules. Generally, FINRA Rules permit the FINRA staff to (a) request the books and records of member firms, and (b) take sworn testimony of firms' associated persons.[4] Further, FINRA member firms and their associated persons are required to respond to a request for information pursuant to FINRA Rules, and failure to do so could result in a fine, suspension,

---

[3]http://www.finra.org/Industry/Compliance/Registration/MemberApplicationProgram/HowtoBecomeaMember/P006269.
[4]FINRA Manual – FINRA Rules, § 8210(a).

or bar from the industry.[5] Under the Exchange Act, within six months of a broker-dealer registering with the SEC, the exchange of which the broker-dealer is a member (FINRA) must examine the broker-dealer to determine that it is operating in conformity with applicable fiscal responsibility rules.[6]

5.2 FINRA'S RISK-BASED APPROACH

In recent years, FINRA has shifted to a risk-based approach for its examinations. FINRA asks firms to complete a Risk Control Assessment to assist them in determining exam priorities. The riskiest firms, according to FINRA's risk profile model, will have a FINRA examination every year. The least risky firms will be examined approximately every four years. FINRA takes many factors into account when determining a firm's risk profile model. For example, FINRA considers a firm's business activities, methods of operation, types of products offered, compliance profile, and the financial condition of the firm.[7]

5.3 FINRA'S REGULATORY AND EXAMINATION PRIORITIES

Every year, FINRA publishes its regulatory and examination priorities to highlight significant risks and issues that could adversely affect investors and market integrity in the coming year. These priorities represent issues that FINRA will incorporate into its examinations or target for reviews. FINRA issued the tenth edition of its Regulatory and Examination Priorities letter in January 2015, setting forth its 2015 regulatory and examination priorities.[8] In this letter, FINRA first described recurring challenges of firms, including putting customers first, firm culture, supervision, risk management and controls,

---

[5] See FINRA Manual at §§ 8210(b), 8310(a).
[6] See 15 U.S.C. § 78o; 17 C.F.R. § 240.15b2-2(b).
[7] http://www.finra.org/newsroom/speeches/ketchum/p120108.
[8] http://www.finra.org/web/groups/industry/@ip/@reg/@guide/documents/industry/p6022 39.pdf.

product and service offerings, and conflicts of interest. With respect to conflicts of interest, FINRA noted that it had recently announced several Enforcement actions against firms for failing to adequately address conflicts of interest.[9]

FINRA also described its areas of focus in 2015, which were divided into Sales Practice, Financial and Operational, and Market Integrity priorities. As part of FINRA's 2015 Sales Practice priorities, FINRA referenced the following areas of focus:

- Product-focused concerns, explaining that firms need to perform due diligence, make sound suitability decisions and describe product risks in a balanced manner that retail investors can understand.

- Interest rate-sensitive fixed income securities, with the instruction that FINRA examiners will look for concentrated positions in products that are highly sensitive to interest rates, such as long-term duration fixed income securities, high yield bonds, mortgage-backed securities, or bond funds composed of interest rate-sensitive securities, and test for suitability and adequate disclosures.

- Variable annuities, which will result in FINRA examiners conducting assessments of compensation structures that improperly incentivize the sale of variable annuities, as well as the suitability of recommendations, statements made about the products, and the adequacy of disclosures made about material features of variable annuities.

- Alternative mutual funds, which, according to FINRA, raise concerns when compared to conventional funds, of customers not understanding the strategy involved or how the funds will respond to various market conditions. FINRA will also focus on whether firms are reviewing alternative funds through their new-product review process.

---

[9]In December 2014, FINRA announced that it had fined 10 firms a total of $43.5 million for allowing their equity research analysts to solicit investment banking business and for offering favorable research coverage in connection with the 2010 planned initial public offering of Toys R Us. http://www.finra.org/Newsroom/NewsReleases/2014/P602059.

- Non-traded private Real Estate Investment Trusts ("REITS"), focusing on risks of lack of liquidity, high fees, and valuation difficulty. FINRA also stated that firms should perform due diligence on an ongoing basis on REITs that their representatives are recommending and look for "red flags" arising from a REIT's financial statements or management approach.[10]

- Exchange Traded Products ("ETPs") tracking alternatively weighted indices, which FINRA states for individual investors, may be complex or unfamiliar and provide exposure to specific investment risk factors or strategies.

- Structured Retail Products ("SRPs"), including structured notes with complex payout structures and using proprietary indices as reference assets. FINRA states it will focus on whether wholesalers have robust know-your-distributor policies and procedures reasonably designed to ensure potential distributors have adequate controls and systems in place and on additional conflict issues that may arise where the distributor and wholesaler are affiliated companies.

- Floating-rate bank loan funds, particularly as they relate to retail investors. FINRA views these funds as difficult to value, with longer settlement times than other investments and relatively illiquid which can pose liquidity challenges if a significant number of investors make redemptions requests at the same time.

---

[10]In March 2014, FINRA announced that it had fined LPL Financial LLC $950,000 for supervisory deficiencies related to the sales of alternative investment products, including non-traded real estate investment trusts, oil and gas partnerships, business development companies ("BDCs"), hedge funds, managed futures, and other illiquid pass-through investments. http://www.finra.org/newsroom/newsreleases/2014/p468052.

In October 2012, FINRA ordered David Lerner Associates, Inc. ("DLA") to pay approximately $12 million in restitution to affected customers who purchased shares in Apple REIT Ten, a non-traded $2 billion REIT DLA sold, and to customers who were charged excessive markups. In addition, FINRA fined David Lerner, DLA's founder, President and CEO, $250,000, and suspended him for one year from the securities industry, followed by a two-year suspension from acting as a principal. FINRA also sanctioned DLA's Head Trader, William Mason, $200,000, and suspended him for six months from the securities industry for his role in charging excessive municipal bond and CMO markups. http://www.finra.org/newsroom/newsreleases/2012/p191729.

- Securities-Backed Lines of Credit ("SBLOCs"), for which broker-dealers should have proper controls in place to supervise. FINRA examiners will scrutinize whether customers are being fully apprised of these program features and whether firms have operational procedures in place that enable them to interact with the lending institution to monitor the customers' accounts, keep adequate records, and ensure that customers are promptly notified when collateral shortfalls occur.

- Supervision rules, which were revised by FINRA in December 2014 and modify numerous requirements, including those relating to: (1) supervising offices of supervisory jurisdiction and inspecting non-branch offices; (2) managing conflicts of interest in a firm's supervisory system; (3) performing risk-based review of correspondence and internal communications; (4) carrying out risk-based review of investment banking and securities transactions; (5) monitoring for insider trading, conducting internal investigations, and reporting related information to FINRA; and (6) testing and verifying supervisory control procedures.[11]

- Individual Retirement Account ("IRA") rollover and other wealth events, with a focus on firms' controls around the handling of wealth events in investors' lives, such as situations where an investor faces a decision about what to do with a large amount of money arising from an inheritance, life insurance payout, sale of a business or other major asset, divorce settlement, or an IRA rollover. FINRA examiners will scrutinize the controls firms have in place related to wealth events, with an emphasis on firms' compliance with their supervisory, suitability, and disclosure obligations.

- Excessive trading and concentration controls, as a result of shortcomings FINRA says it has observed in firms' supervision of quantitative suitability and concentration. FINRA examiners will focus on firms' supervisory processes, systems, and controls concerning how firms monitor for excessive trading and product concentration and will review the criteria for exception reports

---

[11]See, for greater detail on FINRA's new supervision rules, http://www.finra.org/web/groups/industry/@ip/@reg/@notice/documents/notices/p465940.pdf.

that firms use and the adequacy of firms' follow-up on these exceptions.

- Private placements, for which FINRA indicates there are examples of inadequate due diligence and suitability analysis as well as offering documents and communications containing misrepresentations, omissions of material information, or inconsistencies with FINRA's communication rules.
- High-risk and recidivist brokers, which FINRA says cause outsized risk to investors. As a consequence, FINRA is expanding its use of data mining, analytics, specially targeted examinations, and expedited investigations and enforcement actions to respond to these concerns.
- Sales charge discounts and waivers, as a result of FINRA's observation that in some instances customers do not receive the volume discounts (breakpoints) or sales charge waivers to which they are entitled when purchasing products like non-traded REITs, Unit Investment Trusts, Business Development Corporations, and mutual funds.[12]
- Senior investors, which FINRA is trying to protect by having its examiners review carefully communications with seniors, the suitability of investment recommendations made to seniors, the training of registered representatives to handle senior-specific issues, and the supervision firms have in place to protect seniors.
- Anti-money laundering, with a particular focus on certain types of accounts, including Cash Management Accounts ("CMAs") and certain Delivery versus Payment/Receipt versus Payment ("DVP/RVP") accounts, as well as on adequacy of firms' surveillance of customer trading. FINRA also noted that it believes firms' due diligence in microcap securities for AML and section 5 compliance is at times inadequate, regardless of whether they

---

[12]In April 2014, FINRA announced that it had fined Merrill Lynch $8 million for failing to waive mutual fund sales charges for certain charities and retirement accounts and ordered Merrill Lynch to pay $24.4 million in restitution to affected customers, in addition to $64.8 million the firm has already repaid to disadvantaged investors. http://www.finra.org/Newsroom/NewsReleases/2014/P530005.

receive shares from another broker-dealer or transfer agent, and whether in physical form or electronically.[13]

- Municipal advisors and securities, to ensure compliance with the new SEC municipal advisor registration rules that became effective in July 2014.[14]

Financial and Operational priorities disclosed by FINRA included:

- Funding and liquidity: Valuing non-high-quality liquid assets, based upon FINRA's observation that at times firms' funding and liquidity plans rely on being able to sell or enter into repurchase transactions at or very near to the prices at which the firms have marked their inventory to market. As a result, FINRA will examine for the integrity of marks-to-market for such securities and for supervisory controls surrounding the overall valuation process.

- Sales to customers involving tax-exempt or FDIC-Insured products, which should be examined by FINRA for the creation and resolution of short positions, including compliance with possession or control requirements and the adequacy of supervisory processes in place for the expeditious resolution of these positions.

- Cybersecurity, which has also become a priority for the SEC and will result in FINRA examiners reviewing firms' approaches to cybersecurity risk management, including their governance structures and processes for conducting risk assessments and addressing the output of those assessments.

---

[13]In 2014, FINRA fined Brown Brothers Harriman & Co. ("BBH") $8 million for substantial anti-money laundering compliance failures, including its failure to have an adequate anti-money laundering program in place to monitor and detect suspicious penny stock transactions. BBH's former Global AML Compliance Officer Harold Crawford was also fined $25,000 and suspended for one month. http://www.finra.org/Newsroom/NewsReleases/2014/P443442.

[14]For more information about these new municipal advisor registration rules, see http://www.sec.gov/rules/final/2013/34-70462.pdf.

- Outsourcing, which will be a priority area of review during FINRA examinations, and will include an analysis of the due diligence and risk assessment firms perform on potential providers, as well as the supervision they implement for the outsourced activities and functions.
- Investor protection and timely reporting of disclosable information, for which FINRA examiners will review whether required disclosures are complete, accurate, and made within the required time periods; determine whether firms have controls, processes, and procedures in place to ensure timely filings; and determine whether public records reviews are occurring.

Market Integrity priorities included:

- Supervision and governance surrounding trading technology, which will be reviewed by FINRA examination teams with an emphasis on the development and ongoing supervision of algorithms.
- Abusive algorithms, which FINRA attempts to tackle by further enhancing its surveillance program to detect new types of potentially manipulative trading activity brought about through the use of abusive trading algorithms.
- Cross-market and cross-product manipulation, for which FINRA states its cross-market surveillance now covers over 99 percent of the U.S. equity markets.
- Order routing practices, best execution, and disclosure, which led to a sweep that FINRA is conducting of firms that route a significant percentage of their unmarketable customer limit orders to trading venues that provide the highest trading rebates for providing liquidity.
- Market access, for which FINRA plans to commence a pilot program to leverage the relationship trading alert activity detected in its cross-market surveillance program to provide firms with information intended to supplement firms' supervision efforts with respect to detecting and preventing.

- Audit trail integrity, with particular focus on late reporting in TRACE[15]-eligible and municipal securities that appears to result from inadequate processes and procedures on trading desks.

These exam priorities should be reviewed carefully every year prior to the FINRA exam to understand what FINRA examiners are being advised to focus on in their exams.

5.4 DIFFERENCES BETWEEN FINRA AND SEC EXAMS

FINRA's examinations differ from the SEC's in that FINRA has more areas to cover. The SEC's exam will likely be a more thorough review of a limited number of areas.

FINRA examinations are generally routine, cycle exams that cover virtually all the business and operational areas of a firm. According to Matt Dwyer, a recognized expert in FINRA examinations, FINRA's exams have a little more structure to them because of the larger number of areas in which they are examining. Dwyer is the Owner and President of a consulting firm that assists broker-dealers and investment advisers in fulfilling their regulatory and compliance obligations, with a special focus on FINRA exams. He also served as a Senior Compliance Examiner for FINRA for nearly six years. Dwyer notes the SEC might spend 80 percent to 90 percent of their time in one area of a firm's business. FINRA, however, is going to look at numerous different areas regardless of the make-up of the firm.

It is even possible that a firm will face a FINRA exam and shortly thereafter, the SEC will contact the firm and announce its examination as well, or vice versa. Dwyer notes how firms often would prefer having both exams one right after the other, or even at the same time. If the firm wishes to have a break between exams, according to Dwyer, the firm may make a request to FINRA for scheduling flexibility. It is perfectly appropriate for firms to inform FINRA that the initial exam schedule is not convenient because one

---

[15]Trade Reporting and Compliance Engine.

of the firm's key personnel such as a CCO or CFO is unavailable, or on vacation. Dwyer notes that generally FINRA will be flexible about these types of scheduling matters.

5.5 TYPES OF FINRA EXAMS

During a routine examination, FINRA will review the firm's financial condition, supervisory system, internal controls, AML, sales practice issues, business continuity planning, and other operational and business areas. Cycle examinations often focus on the following areas, among others:

- Firms' supervisory control reports, which specify firms' written compliance policies and supervisory procedures and document the testing of these policies.
- Level of experience of a firm's compliance personnel.
- Anti-money laundering (including the adequacy of firms' customer identification processes).
- Trade reports for over-the-counter securities.
- E-mail retention practices.
- Adequacy of books and records.
- Firms' supervision of employees' outside business practices and employee trading.

FINRA also conducts Trading and Financial Compliance ("TFCE") (previously known as Trading and Market Making ("TMMS")) exams which cover trading. Dwyer explains that these exams deal with trade reporting and market making, particularly for firms who have direct access to the market.

Cause examinations can also originate from FINRA's review of customer complaints, employee arbitrations, whistleblower tips, and/or referrals from other regulators. They may be unannounced, and examiners may seek to perform data captures, including trading records, e-mails, and other electronically stored information.

FINRA also does some sweep exams. According to Dwyer, FINRA will look at a certain segment of the industry, a certain handful of firms, or a certain business activity. Dwyer notes that one of the big FINRA sweeps in the past 10 to 15 years was the mutual fund break point examination in which FINRA went to a number of firms and focused solely on that one issue. In 2014, FINRA targeted cybersecurity issues and conducted an assessment of firms' approaches to managing cyber-security threats. FINRA had four broad goals in performing this assessment: (1) understand better the types of threats that firms faced; (2) increase understanding of firms' risk appetite, exposure, and major areas of vulnerability in their IT systems; (3) understand better firms' approaches to managing these threats, including through risk assessment processes, IT protocols, application management practices, and supervision; and (4) share observations and findings with firms.[16]

5.6 CONDUCT OF FINRA EXAMS

FINRA generally will call to announce the exam two to four weeks prior to the on-site visit. Shortly after FINRA announces the exam, the firm will be asked to complete a Web Information Request. The firm will be required to review and update information that FINRA keeps regarding your firm. After the Web Information Request has been completed, FINRA will use this information as well as other information to produce a Records Request List.

The length of time examiners spend with a firm varies greatly depending on size. Large, international firms will find that examiners often stay on-site for three to four months. For a mid-size firm, according to Dwyer, they may be on site for one to two weeks.

Dwyer advises that prior to the FINRA exam, firms should review their supervisory control (3120) report, which is due March 31 of every year, for potential weaknesses. Dwyer counsels that a risk assessment should then be conducted and basic testing done to determine the vulnerabilities prior to the exam. If weaknesses or deficiencies are identified, a mock exam can be conducted and efforts can be made to remedy the deficiencies prior to FINRA's arrival. Dwyer

---

[16]See   http://www.finra.org/Industry/Regulation/Guidance/TargetedExaminationLetters/
P443219.

advises firms to at least initially provide only a high-level summary of the internal review or exam that the firm conducts. According to Dwyer, giving FINRA the entire report may actually provide the examiners with a "treasure map" for deficiencies. Dwyer notes that, in general, firms should not volunteer documentation to FINRA, but only produce something if specifically requested.

Once notified of a FINRA exam, a records request will be made by FINRA, electronically, through FINRA's gateway. Dwyer advises that the point person for the exam should separately meet with anyone who is going to produce records or that FINRA may wish to interview. The point person should provide the employees with a copy of the document request and obtain an estimate date for when the documents will be available. It is also important to track each FINRA request and the content of the response. Dwyer notes that there are times during an exam where the FINRA examiner will say "Oh, yeah, can I see that month's worth of statements?" or "Can you add such and such to the list?" In that scenario, Dwyer advises that the firm contact ask for FINRA to put the request in writing or ask for it electronically so that it can be effectively tracked. While Dwyer notes that FINRA has improved in this area in the last few years and currently the vast majority of requests made by examiners are electronic, there remain exceptions where the firm should seek the information in writing.

Dwyer explains that the firm's point of contact should sit in on every meeting or interview conducted by the examiners. He notes that, ordinarily, counsel would not participate in these meetings. However, Dwyer points out that in a smaller firm where the CCO is also a lawyer or even the firm's General Counsel, it would be perfectly acceptable for the lawyer to attend every meeting or interview.

Dwyer recommends that the firm's point of contact play an active role in interviews conducted by the FINRA examiners. He notes that, for example, if the examiners are speaking to the firm's head of trading and they ask him or her something about trade reporting of which the head of trading has little knowledge, the point of contact should interject and say, for example, that trade reporting is ultimately the responsibility of the operations division and "you're going to want to talk to the head of operations about that." Dwyer notes that an active role may go too far if, for example, the FINRA examiner states something to the effect that "I need so-and-so to answer the question, not you." In that scenario, the point of contact should back off so as not to antagonize the examiner. It is important to balance the line between keeping a good relationship with the examiners and protecting the employee interacting with the examiners.

Dwyer explains that from time to time, firms have to deal with difficult examiners. He notes that, generally, there will be a lead examiner and potentially, two or three other examiners on site. If one has a problem with a specific examiner, Dwyer advises the firm to speak to that specific examiner first. Dwyer notes that the most common problem that firms have with FINRA examiners is when the examiners take it upon themselves to explore the firm and ask questions of people without permission or scheduling a time. In that case, Dwyer counsels that one should speak to the examiner who has been acting in that way and say, "We'll get you everything you need but it has to come through me for a couple of reasons. First, those people have a job to do. Second, I need to be able to track all your requests and log those and third, those were the ground rules we set up at the kick-off meeting." If that does not work, Dwyer advises going to the lead examiner in confidence, and letting them know about the issue with the more junior examiner. If the lead examiner does not resolve the problem, Dwyer says that one should not be afraid to contact the lead examiner's supervisor who is usually not on-site but back at FINRA's home offices and advise him or her of the situation.

Dwyer explains that it is possible or even likely that the FINRA examiner will have less experience than an SEC examiner as the position of SEC examiner is a more prestigious one than that of FINRA examiner. With FINRA, a firm may be faced with a very inexperienced examiner such as a recent college graduate who is intelligent but does not have the industry experience.[17] In that scenario, Dwyer advises that the firm may spend a great deal of time explaining to them, for example, about trade reporting in a very basic manner. In

---

[17]While this scenario may also occur with an SEC examiner, it is more likely to happen in a FINRA exam.

these situations, it is important to be patient with the examiner and not come across as obnoxious or act as if the examiner is wasting the firm's time.

Dwyer notes that a benefit of checking in with the FINRA examiners often during the course of the exam is that they may provide a heads-up of a potential deficiency that they are looking at prior to the exit conference. If that occurs, the firm has an opportunity to address the concern on the part of the examiners before it gets escalated at their end. Dwyer advises that the firm contact discuss the potential finding with the examiner and even potentially bring in a subject-matter expert to the discussion, if necessary. The firm should do its research before challenging the examiner and trying to convince them that their initial impression may be erroneous.

Dwyer gives the example of a potential FINRA finding about a suitability sale, noting that suitability is notoriously a tough violation to prove because the suitability rule is fairly vague, and therefore he advises firms to push back against these types of findings. Dwyer counsels that in such cases, where the firm feels strongly that the examiner is wrong, one might consider gathering all their research and information and contacting the supervisor at the FINRA office during the field work. It may even be worthwhile to include the firm's senior management and General Counsel in this effort.

Even though the field work may be over, the exam should not be viewed as concluded. Regulatory staff often will take the documentation back to their offices for further review and analysis. Additional information requests may be received for some time after the field work is done.

5.7 HOW THE FINRA EXAM CONCLUDES

FINRA examinations conclude in one of four dispositions:

- **No further action:** No violations have been cited. This disposition is somewhat rare.
- **Cautionary action:** This is the most common type of disposition. In this case, one has generally between 30 and 60 days to make the changes FINRA is requesting. According to Dwyer, in

the firm's next Rule 3120 annual testing, it is important for the firm to re-test any areas mentioned in the Cautionary Action to ensure that the deficiency has been rectified.

- **Compliance conference:** This indicates that FINRA is concerned about the firm's overall compliance and supervisory structure or that major issues exist in critical business or operational areas. Although this is an informal action and does not have to be publicly disclosed, it is a serious matter. According to Dwyer, this result of a FINRA exam is becoming less common and would generally only occur if the firm had received Cautionary Actions about the same issue on several occasions, and FINRA believes that these actions are not being taken seriously. If this occurs, the next exam will likely be more rigorous.

- **Enforcement Referral:** The last type of disposition is where the examiners tell the firm "We have referred this to our Enforcement department." In this scenario, counsel should be retained immediately. Counsel retained should be very familiar with FINRA and how it operates. Dwyer notes that even good firms are fined by FINRA. He explains that, for example, many AML violations result in an enforcement referral. In addition, according to Dwyer, during a TMMS examination, trade reporting errors often result in Enforcement referrals.

Dwyer notes that there are times where only a portion of the examiners' findings are referred to Enforcement and the remaining issues are dealt with through a deficiency letter. Dwyer explains that there are also occasions where the final disposition of an exam is delayed, pointing to one case where FINRA closed off the exam field work in March and over six months later, they had not provided a final disposition to the exam. Dwyer notes that FINRA generally strives to have a disposition within 90 to180 days from the end of the field work, but is not always successful.

5.8 EDUCATING THE FINRA EXAMINERS

As discussed above, FINRA exams may be broader and less sophisticated than SEC exams and firms should be prepared accordingly.

FINRA examiners will make every effort to check each box of areas they are required to examine, and will focus on the larger FINRA priorities for that year. While it is often difficult to avoid a few technical deficiencies or mistakes, firms should be prepared to educate FINRA examiners and be patient with them as they learn the firm's business and industry. In most instances, firms like broker-dealers will be able to avoid major problems or referrals to Enforcement as long as their policies and procedures are in place and up-to-date and they follow applicable rules and guidelines. If the FINRA examiners insist that something is a violation even after the firm point of contact has tried to explain the actual situation to them, it may be worth retaining a FINRA compliance consultant and escalating the matter to higher-level FINRA staff. However, in most cases such as cyclical FINRA exams, it is best to accept minor issues being raised, put in place remedial measures promptly and appropriately, and move on from the exam.

CHAPTER 6

How to Defend an NFA Examination

The CFTC is the independent Agency of the U.S. government that regulates futures and options markets and administers the CEA, 7 U.S.C. section 1, *et seq.*, which prohibits fraudulent conduct in the trading of futures contracts. With a few exceptions, all individuals and firms that intend to do business as futures professionals must register under the CEA.

In addition, those individuals and firms that wish to conduct futures-related business with the public must apply for membership with the NFA, the SRO for the U.S. futures industry. The NFA states that it "strives every day to safeguard market integrity, protect investors and help our Members meet their regulatory responsibilities."[1]

6.1 TYPES OF ENTITIES UNDER THE JURISDICTION OF THE NFA

Many diverse types of entities are subject to regulation under the CEA and are required to register with the NFA. These include:

- FCMs, defined as an individual or organization that does both of the following:

---

[1] http://www.nfa.futures.org/index.asp.

- Solicits or accepts orders to buy or sell futures contracts, options on futures, retail off-exchange forex contracts, or swaps;
- Accepts money or other assets from customers to support such orders.[2]
- Swap dealers, defined as any person who holds themselves out as a dealer in swaps (meaning that they stand prepared to enter swap deals):
  - Makes a market in swaps;
  - Regularly enters into swaps with counterparties; or
  - Engages in any activity causing the person to be commonly known as a dealer or market maker in swaps, with a *de minimis* exception.[3]
- Major swap participants, defined as any person that satisfies any one of the following qualifications:
  - If they maintain a "substantial position" in any Major Swap Category, including positions held for hedging or mitigating risk, or positions maintained by certain employee benefit plans for hedging or mitigating risk;
  - If the swaps create "substantial counterparty exposure" that could threaten the U.S. banking system or financial market stability;
  - If the entity is highly leveraged based on the amount of capital that the entity holds, and that is not subject to capital requirements established by a federal banking Agency.[4]
- Retail Foreign Exchange Dealer ("RFED"), defined as an individual or organization that acts, or offers to act, as a counterparty to an off-exchange foreign currency transaction with a person who is not an eligible contract participant, and the transaction is either:
  - A futures contract, an option on a futures contract, or an option contract (except options traded on a securities exchange); or

---

[2]http://www.nfa.futures.org/NFA-registration/fcm/index.HTML.
[3]http://www.cftclaw.com/2012/04/cftc-approves-rule-defining-swap-dealer/.
[4]Ibid.

- Offered or entered into, on a leveraged or margined basis, or financed by the offeror, counterparty, or person acting in concert with the offeror or counterparty on a similar basis.[5]
- Introducing Broker ("IB"), defined as an individual or organization that solicits or accepts orders to buy or sell futures contracts, options on futures, retail off-exchange forex contracts, or swaps but does not accept money or other assets from customers to support such orders.[6]
- Commodity Pool Operator ("CPO"), defined as an individual or organization that operates a commodity pool and solicits funds for that commodity pool. A commodity pool is an enterprise in which funds contributed by a number of persons are combined for the purpose of trading futures contracts, options on futures, retail off-exchange forex contracts or swaps, or to invest in another commodity pool.[7]
- Commodity Trading Advisor ("CTA"), defined as an individual or organization that, for compensation or profit, advises others as to the value of or the advisability of buying or selling futures contracts, options on futures, retail off-exchange forex contracts, or swaps. Providing advice includes exercising trading authority over a customer's account as well as giving advice based upon knowledge of or tailored to a customer's particular commodity interest account, particular commodity interest trading activity, or other similar types of information.[8]

In addition, Associated Persons ("APs"), who solicit orders, customers, or customer funds (or who supervise persons) on behalf of an FCM, RFED, IB, CTA, or CPO; principals of registered firms; floor brokers; and floor traders also have certain registration requirements.[9]

---

[5] http://www.nfa.futures.org/NFA-registration/rfed/index.HTML.
[6] http://www.nfa.futures.org/NFA-registration/ib/index.HTML.
[7] http://www.nfa.futures.org/NFA-registration/cpo/index.HTML.
[8] http://www.nfa.futures.org/NFA-registration/cta/index.HTML.
[9] http://www.nfa.futures.org/NFA-registration/index.HTML.

6.2 IMPACT OF THE DODD-FRANK ACT

The Dodd-Frank Act had a significant impact on several of the above entities subject to NFA registration. The Dodd-Frank Act significantly expanded the reach of the CFTC by giving it authority over the broadly defined OTC derivatives (swaps) markets, which was then delegated to the NFA for registration purposes. The CFTC, in February 2012, also adopted final rules rescinding an exemption (Rule 4.13(a)(4)) from registration as a commodity pool operator (otherwise known as the "sophisticated investor" exemption) relied upon by many hedge fund and private equity fund managers.[10] In addition, CFTC rules limited the exemptions from registration for CTAs.

6.3 NFA EXAMINATION PROCESS

The NFA strives to conduct examinations of new member firms within a year of the firm becoming active, and is required to examine FCMs and RFEDs on an annual basis if they hold customer funds. According to Deborah Monson, a partner at the law firm of Ropes & Gray and a recognized expert in NFA examinations, because of the significant expansion of the CFTC and NFA's jurisdictions as a result of the Dodd-Frank Act, the NFA's routine exams of new members that previously would occur within 12 months of the firm's registration date, may now occur in the 12- to 24-month time frame. Monson, who received her undergraduate degree from Princeton University and her law degree from the University of Michigan law school, focuses her practice on commodities law, asset management, and private investment funds. She has represented registered and exempt commodity pool operators and commodity trading advisors for nearly 30 years, and regularly advises mutual funds, banks, insurance companies, endowments, and foundations on commodities law matters.

---

[10]http://www.cftc.gov/ucm/groups/public/@newsroom/documents/file/federalregister0209 12b.pdf.

After the initial examination, according to Monson, the NFA will strive to conduct another exam within three to five years. However, the NFA has refocused to a risk-based analysis to determine which of its other registered firms to visit in any given period. Monson says that risk factors that have been traditionally looked at by the NFA, such as customer complaints, concerns during reviews of the website, promotional materials, and referrals from exchanges or the SEC, have increased, and the NFA is now also looking at assets under management, degree of leverage, the types of investments a firm is making, as well as its performance returns. Monson notes that either a firm's too high or too low performance can get the NFA's attention. She says the NFA is also looking at the footnotes in financial statements as well as websites, industry publications, and databases that could provide useful information. Monson notes that the NFA even "googles" companies to search for information that might give rise to risk factors.

The NFA has stated that it intends to visit CPOs, CTAs, and IBs every three to four years, but the frequency may vary depending on its risk analysis.[11] The NFA has also announced for swap dealers and major swap participants that their examinations would begin in the summer of 2014, and would focus on the role and function of the firm's Chief Compliance Officer.[12] The NFA indicated they would arrive on-site 30 days after an initial letter was sent out, and would remain on-site for approximately three weeks.[13] The NFA also indicated it will focus initially on U.S. swap dealers and major swap participants and while it has acknowledged the logistical difficulties in conducting on-site exams of foreign swap dealers and major swap participants, it has not ruled out such exams in the future.[14]

The NFA is also developing a monitoring program for swap dealers and major swap participants which will focus on identifying significant developments at a firm, in an effort by the NFA to get to know these new registrants. This monitoring will occur through a

---

[11] See http://www.nfa.futures.org/NFA-faqs/compliance-faqs/examinations/index.HTML.

[12] See https://www.nfa.futures.org/NFA-compliance/NFA-education-training/NFA-podcasts/TranscriptSDExaminationTeleconference.pdf.

[13] See ibid.

[14] See ibid.

combination of meetings and the review of reports filed by member firms with the CFTC. The NFA plans to meet with CCOs who can involve other individuals as needed. It will use information that it learns from the monitoring program to prioritize examinations and to conduct ad hoc inquiries or investigations.

6.4 PREPARING FOR AN NFA EXAM

Monson explains that in preparing for an NFA exam, the first place to start is NFA's self-examination check list, which is available on the NFA's website.[15] Firms are required to fill out the checklist and the NFA will request the completed checklist when they arrive for the exam. Monson notes that the checklist is not only tied to NFA rules, but also best practices, and it gives firms an indication of what the NFA expects to see when they arrive for the exam. Monson states that it is prudent for firms to have counsel review the completed self-examination checklist as some of the applicability of the questions is not entirely clear and the NFA will be looking at the checklist closely during the exam.

Monson also says that it is relatively common for firms to do mock exams prior to the NFA's arrival, noting two different approaches to preparing for NFA exams. One approach is to hire an outside compliance consultant or law firm and have a full-blown outside mock audit. This route is a good idea if firm management is legitimately concerned about deficiencies or areas that may not be in compliance. The second approach according to Monson is to utilize the pre-audit questionnaire that the NFA sends firms seeking information for its exam, such as the identification of employee responsibilities and affiliates, their qualifications, information concerning the firm's client base and service providers and internal policies, procedures, and an organizational chart. With the pre-audit questionnaire, a firm can anticipate some aspects of the NFA exam, and can conduct a "fire drill internal audit" based on this information.

---

[15] See http://www.nfa.futures.org/NFA-compliance/publication-library/self-exam-question naire.HTML.

Monson explains that the length of the routine exams depends on how the firm answers the pre-audit questionnaire. The amount of time on-site, according to Monson, may vary from a few days to a few weeks, depending upon the complexity of the firm. Generally, Monson says, the NFA will send between three and five examiners. After the on-site portion, the NFA examiners will return to the offices and continue their review with the materials they have obtained from the firm. The NFA has five months to issue its report.

6.5 LENGTH AND CONDUCT OF THE NFA EXAM

In terms of how the NFA conducts its exams, Monson notes that the NFA examiners have a template and will almost always look at certain areas, such as: (1) firm and principal registration, checking if the firm as well as the individuals listed as principals on the firm's form ADV are properly registered; (2) associated persons, to determine if they are all properly registered; (3) branch offices; (4) promotional materials; (5) supervisory policies and procedures; (6) trading and allocation policies; (7) financial reporting and records; (8) corporate documents; and (9) ethics training procedures and proof of completion.

Monson explains that the NFA ordinarily begins the exam with an opening interview, providing an opportunity for the firm to put together an opening presentation that presents its history, describes its business and, as importantly, describes what its business does not do. The firm should then designate a contact person to answer questions and provide information throughout the exam. The NFA generally e-mails out questions and requests as they arise to the firm's contact person. It will also ask to interview employees and the contact person should manage that as well to determine the scope.

Monson advises that requests for information from NFA examiners should be responded to promptly as the longer the NFA examiners are waiting for information, the more opportunity they may have to think about new things to request. Monson further counsels that if firms do not have the information, it is better to be upfront with the NFA and simply say, "We don't have the answer right now but we will get it right away." When providing information or documentation to the NFA examiners, Monson explains that firms can address issues or concerns about the information or documentation provided. Monson notes that NFA examiners, unlike SEC examiners, will often raise questions as they learn about the firm during the examination. These discussions give the firm an opportunity to explain why perhaps what they are doing is perfectly legal and within the regulations. In the alternative, Monson explains that firms can acknowledge to the NFA examiners, if appropriate, that something was done improperly, but it was inadvertent and isolated; the steps taken to ensure that the problem does not re-occur can also be explained at that time. In this scenario, firms can resolve matters prior to them being announced as a deficiency and raised in the exit interview.

Given the ability to address issues during the course of the NFA exam, it may be wise to consult with outside counsel, according to Monson, to obtain assistance with discussions with NFA examiners. Monson explains that, depending on the circumstances, it may be advisable for outside counsel to remain in the background and not interact directly with the NFA examiners, but merely to provide the firm's contact person with guidance and information.

Monson also suggests that firms be strong advocates for their positions, but not confrontational in interacting with the NFA examiners. In providing documents to the examiners, the firm may include in the e-mail an explanation of the document and the firm's interpretation of the issue being raised by the NFA. Many times Monson says language for these explanatory e-mails will come from outside counsel. She also notes that she has found, generally, that NFA examiners are willing to listen to explanations provided by firms and are flexible in terms of trying to see something from the firm's perspective.

Monson describes common mistakes that firms subject to regulation by the NFA make that lead to issues in an NFA exam. One example is the NFA's Bylaw 1101, which prohibits NFA members from doing business with most non-members that are required to be registered with the CFTC as an FCM, IB, CPO, or CTA.[16] The

---

[16] See http://www.nfa.futures.org/NFA-faqs/compliance-faqs/bylaw-1101/index.HTML.

NFA further requires, according to Monson, that firms conduct due diligence to determine if they are doing business with anyone who is supposed to be an NFA member but is not. Firms are also required to document their review and due diligence. A second example of this is seen surrounding the topic of ethics training. Monson explains that the NFA requires anyone who is registered as an associated person to have initial ethics training and then follow-up periodic ethics training with prescribed topics. Ethics training is an area, according to Monson, that the NFA will likely scrutinize in an exam. The NFA will request the firm's organizational chart and compare it to records of who is registered and seek to ensure that all appropriate training has been conducted. Monson adds how the NFA has particular rules with regard to advertising, including that each piece of promotional material has to be approved in writing by a supervisor that is not the same person who prepared the materials. The NFA will inquire about written records showing compliance in this area on an exam.

6.6 HOW THE NFA EXAM CONCLUDES

Monson describes the following as possible outcomes of an NFA exam: (1) a letter saying the examination has concluded without findings; (2) the deficiency letter; and (3) a referral to the NFA's Enforcement Division. Monson says in general, a "no findings" letter is not as rare in an NFA exam as it is in an SEC exam. The deficiency letter would include a summary of examination findings as well as, potentially, supervisory or internal control weaknesses. The letters arrive at the end of the NFA exam. Monson explains that once the deficiency letter is issued, the firm generally has 10 business days to respond. This timeline may be difficult according to Monson, as the firm's response should document the steps taken to correct the deficiencies with supporting materials. Monson explains that if, for instance, the NFA concludes that a firm's promotional materials are misleading, the firm must revise all the materials and show that they have remediated its processes and procedures within the

10-business-day time frame. This is another reason to have the dialogue with the NFA early so that the firm has a better sense of the issues that may appear in a deficiency letter.

Monson explains that if the firm still believes the NFA's findings are inaccurate, they are not precluded from continuing to assert their position even after a deficiency letter has been issued. It is a cost–benefit analysis for the firm to determine if it is worth remediating the issues that the NFA has raised or attempting to change their minds. Monson says that she has seen situations, although not very many, where firms have responded to deficiency letters with arguments challenging the NFA findings. She also has seen instances where the NFA agreed to resolve the matter to the firm's satisfaction after the firm continued to advocate its position even after the deficiency letter was issued.

Monson further advises that if the firm chooses to respond to the deficiency letter with proof that the underlying problem has been remedied, the firm should also follow up with the NFA to request confirmation that they have accepted and are satisfied with the firm's response. The deficiency letter will be a major component of what the NFA considers when it conducts its next exam of the firm and consequently, according to Monson, the firm should review the letter to confirm that there are no lingering issues before the next exam. If the NFA finds similar issues in the next exam that had already been included in a deficiency letter, Monson advises that the NFA is more likely to refer the second violation to Enforcement.

6.7 CFTC EXAMINATIONS

Monson notes that the CFTC also conducts exams, although not nearly as frequently as the NFA. According to Monson, CFTC exams are quite different from NFA exams. In Monson's experience, CFTC examiners on occasion seek to meet with firm representatives for a short period of time in an informational type setting. In a very rare situation, the CFTC may be involved if there are serious violations at a firm or where customer money is at risk, and the CFTC, together with the Department of Justice and perhaps the FBI, may need to take over the firm, as was the case with MF Global.[17]

Monson counsels that firms used to having SEC exams that are newly under CFTC and NFA jurisdiction should not be repurposing their SEC materials and trying to tailor them for NFA oversight. She stresses that the CFTC/NFA rules are different from the SEC's. The NFA's focus in exams is unique and firms should be careful that materials they are taking out of their files and producing in an NFA exam are appropriately tailored and repurposed and properly reflecting the CFTC/NFA regime.

6.8 FOCUSING ON STRICT COMPLIANCE WITH THE REGULATIONS

In defending NFA and CFTC examinations, firms should ensure that they are in compliance with even the minutest details of the regulations. For the most part, firms should be aware of the areas of focus by the NFA or CFTC and have the opportunity to remedy any compliance issues prior to the exam. Attention to detail is critical to satisfying NFA and CFTC examiners. As it is not always possible in every situation to ensure perfect compliance, where the NFA or CFTC examiner finds a deficiency, it is advisable to simply acknowledge the errors, put them in the proper perspective, and ensure that they are fixed by the next exam.

---

[17]MF Global filed a voluntary petition for bankruptcy under Chapter 11 on October 31, 2011 after the firm found itself unable to finance its short-term obligations and after significant discussions and consultations with the CFTC. See http://www.cftc.gov/ucm/groups/public/@aboutcftc/documents/file/oigregulationmfglobal.pdf.

CHAPTER 7

How to Defend SEC Enforcement Actions

I n some instances, the adverse effects of a difficult examination can lead not only to deficiency letters but could also result in a referral to the division, or department of the Agency, or SRO that conducts the Enforcement functions for an investigation and, potentially, an Enforcement action. The next four chapters describe how companies can defend first, investigations and second, Enforcement actions brought by the SEC, FINRA, CFTC, and NFA.

7.1 SEC'S LAW ENFORCEMENT FUNCTION

The SEC is a law enforcement Agency and its Enforcement Division executes this law enforcement function by investigating securities law violations, and by making recommendations to the SEC Commission to first conduct these investigations, and then to bring civil actions in federal court or before an administrative law judge on behalf of the SEC Commission. The SEC's Enforcement Division also coordinates with law enforcement Agencies, such as the DOJ with respect to criminal actions brought for securities law violations. The DOJ may seek indictments for criminal violations of securities laws on their own initiative or through referrals from the SEC.

The SEC identifies the following common violations that may lead to SEC investigations as:

- Misrepresentation or omission of information considered significant or important about securities.
- Manipulating the market prices of securities.
- Stealing customers' funds or securities.
- Violating broker-dealers' responsibility to treat customers fairly.
- Insider trading (violating a trust relationship by trading on material, non-public information about a security).
- Selling unregistered securities.[1]

When bringing a civil action, the SEC will file a complaint with a U.S. District Court and ask the court for a sanction or remedy, such as an injunction, that prohibits any further violations of law or SEC rules, and civil monetary penalties, or the return of illegal profits (called disgorgement). The court may also bar or suspend an individual from serving as a corporate officer or director.

In an administrative matter, the actions are heard by an administrative law judge, who works for the SEC. The administrative law judge presides over a hearing and considers the evidence presented by the SEC Enforcement staff, as well as any evidence submitted by the defendant. Following the hearing, the administrative law judge issues an initial decision that contains a recommended sanction. Both the Enforcement staff and the defendant may appeal all or any portion of the initial decision to the full Commission (i.e., the SEC Chairman and its Commissioners). The Commission may affirm the decision of the administrative law judge, reverse the decision, or remand it for additional hearings. Administrative sanctions include cease and desist orders, suspension or revocation of broker-dealer and investment advisor registrations, censures, bars from association with the securities industry, civil monetary penalties, and disgorgement.

---

[1] See http://www.sec.gov/News/Article/Detail/Article/1356125787012#.VG4YJdhOW70.

7.2 HOW SEC ENFORCEMENT ACTIONS ARE TRIGGERED

Bradley J. Bondi, a partner and leader of the Securities Enforcement practice at the law firm of Cahill Gordon & Reindel in Washington, D.C. and a recognized expert in SEC Enforcement cases, who served as Counsel to two SEC Commissioners, Troy Paredes and Paul Atkins, and as Deputy General Counsel and Assistant Director of the Financial Crisis Inquiry Commission ("FCIC"), a bipartisan commission established by Congress to investigate the causes of the financial crisis, states that SEC inquiries or actions may be triggered by the following different activities:

- Abnormal activity in a company's disclosures, such as an unexpected announcement made regarding earnings or the termination of a long-term contract, or any unusual changes in an organization of management or unexpected resignation of an officer.
- Shareholder litigation that may be filed against a company alleging a violation of federal securities law.
- A whistleblower, or someone that provides a tip or information to the SEC about a potential security law violation.
- The self-disclosure by a company to the SEC of a potential violation of the federal securities laws.
- Information from other law enforcement or regulators, such as the DOJ, state regulators, state attorneys general, other regulators like the CFTC, or foreign regulators such as the UK Serious Fraud Office.

Companies, their officers, and directors may be subject to criminal prosecution, SEC Enforcement investigations, and actions, and additional actions by other state and federal governmental Agencies as well as SROs. Parallel criminal proceedings alongside SEC Enforcement actions are not unusual. In addition to the logistical problems raised by simultaneous investigations or litigations, a party subject to parallel proceedings faces the additional issue that information gathered by the SEC during an Enforcement investigation may be provided to federal and/or state authorities.

7.3 COMMENCEMENT OF AN SEC ENFORCEMENT ACTION

Frequently, an SEC Enforcement investigation will begin as an informal inquiry, referred to as a Matter Under Inquiry ("MUI"). In these informal investigations, the SEC does not have subpoena power and therefore any appearance or production of documents is voluntary. The investigation can be closed by the Enforcement staff member and the matter is over. Interviews are voluntary in nature; although when conducted, they are often under oath and a transcript will be created. At the interview, the SEC will provide the witness with SEC Form 1662, entitled "Supplemental Information for Persons Supplying Information Voluntarily or Directed to Supply Information."[2] This form explains, among other things, that the witness must provide truthful information and that he or she has a right to purchase a copy of the transcript. Documents can also be requested in an informal inquiry. Most companies cooperate with the SEC during an informal inquiry and spend their time conducting their own internal investigation. Bondi suggests that companies treat an informal request from the SEC for documents with the same level of seriousness as a formal subpoena. According to Bondi, the company usually should respond and cooperate with the SEC. At the same time, Bondi recommends that the company may wish to initiate its own investigation to try to understand what, if any, problems might have occurred that gave rise to the SEC's inquiry.

At this juncture, the company may also wish to consider reaching out to potential witnesses from both inside and outside the company in order to fully understand the potential evidence that the SEC has or will gather in the case. As part of this process, Bondi explains that it is important to understand and distinguish between employee witnesses who have their interests aligned with the company, and potential witnesses who may have exposure or liability themselves. Bondi emphasizes the importance of this distinction because witnesses who are true company witnesses are usually able to be represented by the same counsel that is representing the company. On the other hand,

---

[2]See SEC Form 1662 found at http://www.sec.gov/about/forms/sec1662.pdf.

if it appears as though a potential witness has interests that are adverse to the company because they may themselves be susceptible to being charged by the SEC, Bondi recommends that this person obtain their own counsel. Bondi notes that it behooves the company and the company's counsel to try to steer or help that person in finding their own counsel. Bondi warns that one has to be careful never to obstruct the SEC's investigation. He explains that there is nothing that prevents counsel from being an advocate for their client and that can include reaching out to company witnesses ahead of time, interviewing those company witnesses, understanding what the person knows, understanding the facts, and being in a position to be able to defend the client. However, according to Bondi, counsel must be careful never to cross the line from being an advocate to actually obstructing the SEC investigation by coaching a witness *what* to say as opposed to *how* to say it. Bondi explains that the general rule is that one may always advise witnesses on how to say things, but never what to say.

Bondi also mentions that one of the consequences of the SEC's failures to uncover several high-profile frauds in recent years, including Bernie Madoff's $50 billion Ponzi scheme, is that the SEC Enforcement staff has become very thorough in its document requests and they often will request far more documents than they want or need right away. As a result of this approach, Bondi explains that the Enforcement staff is open and willing to negotiate, to some extent, about the scope of a request and sometimes will allow a defendant, if not to narrow the request, at least to prioritize the productions. By prioritizing the productions the Enforcement staff will educate themselves on the issues and facts involved in their investigation, and perhaps later on will limit the extent of the information it is requesting.

7.4 CONVERTING THE INQUIRY TO A FORMAL INVESTIGATION

At the conclusion of the inquiry, the SEC has the option of simply closing the matter, or attempting to convert it into a formal investigation. If they wish to have it converted into a formal investigation, the

SEC Enforcement staff makes that request to the SEC Commission and it is the Commission that issues the formal order of investigation. The process begins with an Action Memorandum prepared by the staff and sent to the Commission requesting that a formal order of investigation be issued. The formal order includes a description of the violations of the federal securities laws and cites the statutes and rules at issue. It also designates the specific SEC Enforcement staff members who will be conducting the investigation and will have the authority to issue subpoenas. Unlike an informal MUI, a formal investigation can only be closed by senior SEC Enforcement personnel.

7.5 DISCOVERY CONDUCTED BY THE SEC

After a formal order of investigation is issued, the defendant will often receive a subpoena for testimony and documents. Immediately on receipt of the subpoena, steps should be taken to preserve any potentially responsive materials. It is important to comply fully with any SEC subpoena or else attempt to negotiate the modification of the subpoena. Often the SEC Enforcement staff will grant a request for extension of the time to respond to a subpoena. The parties will agree to so-called "rolling productions," particularly where the subpoena is very broad. In this scenario, the materials are produced in groups over time. This agreement gives the defendant more time to gather the materials and also allows the Enforcement staff the opportunity to review the documents. Privileged documents need not be produced and a privilege log is often prepared which provides some identification of the type of document that is being withheld from the SEC on the basis of privilege.

A subpoena also will routinely be issued compelling persons to appear for testimony. Most often, the testimony occurs in the city where the SEC Enforcement staff is located. Defendants may request that the testimony occur in another location more convenient for the witness or their counsel. According to Bondi, if witnesses being subpoenaed are the defendant company's employees, one usually is given a schedule for the order in which the SEC Enforcement staff wish to take their testimony. He explains that companies usually do have some leeway with the Enforcement staff to negotiate a schedule for the interviews, but they may have to occur in a certain order. Bondi explains that the SEC staff will often work up to a certain witness, trying to lay a foundation for a particular deposition by taking the testimony of other witnesses ahead of time. In those instances, Bondi explains that companies may have some leeway with the timing, but not the order of the interviews. He also notes that, generally, defendants will have some advance notice of the interviews, although it may only be for a few weeks' worth of witnesses. For the most part, Bondi says that the SEC realizes that witnesses require preparation from counsel and sometimes that means working with the counsel's schedule.

The SEC rules allow a witness to obtain a copy of the transcript for the testimony and are entitled to nominal witness fees and expenses. The SEC does not believe in "subjects" or "targets" of their investigations, and therefore, defendants will not be specifically informed of their role in the investigation.[3] It is advisable for a witness to be prepared as much as possible prior to giving testimony through a review of the formal order and any relevant documents unearthed in the company's internal investigation or preparation efforts. If the SEC Enforcement staff member shows the witness a document during the testimony, counsel should make sure that the witness has ample opportunity to review the document before answering any questions.

7.6 THE SEC ENFORCEMENT'S "WELLS" PROCESS

After the SEC Enforcement staff conducts its investigation, they prepare a recommendation to the SEC Commission regarding a proposed Enforcement action. As with the request for a formal order, the recommendation will be contained in an Action Memorandum which describes the facts and the law and explains the SEC's case

---

[3]Often it is not that difficult to determine who is the subject or target of the SEC investigation even without the SEC naming the individual in that way.

against the defendant. Generally, before preparing this Action Memorandum, the SEC will give the defendant an opportunity to defend his or her position in what is known as a "Wells"[4] process. This process is generally initiated with a "Wells" notice provided by the SEC to the defendant indicating that the SEC intends to recommend to the Commission that the defendant be sued. The "Wells" notice or letter will often include the statutory sections alleged to have been violated and briefly describe the alleged improper conduct and the remedies being sought. The receipt of a "Wells" notice may trigger public disclosure obligations (particularly for public companies or regulated investment entities).

The defendant then has the opportunity to respond to the SEC with a "Wells" submission and/or request a "Wells" conference wherein the defendant and his or her counsel can provide an oral presentation of why they believe charges should not be brought against the defendant. There are risks to making a "Wells" submission in that the submission is admissible against the party in the Enforcement case and can provide the SEC with a blueprint of the party's anticipated defense strategy. It can also be shared by the SEC with other regulators, including criminal authorities, and may be discoverable by private parties in litigations.

Bondi states that while there are some instances where companies should not make a "Wells" submission, they are very rare, and companies do so at their own peril. Bondi explains that the "Wells" process represents the defendant's opportunity to submit its case to the SEC and not making a "Wells" submission is tantamount to saying that one recognizes that he or she is not planning to provide a defense to the charges. Bondi further explains that those instances where it is not advisable to make a "Wells" submission involve circumstances where the defendant is an individual as opposed to a company, and there are other parties out there looking to take action against that individual as well, whether they are criminal authorities, another civil regulator, foreign regulators, foreign law enforcement, or plaintiffs contemplating bringing class action or other lawsuits.

---

[4] The "Wells" process, which includes a "Wells" notice and "Wells" submission or conference, is named after John Wells, the former SEC Committee Chair who first pioneered this process in 1972.

The "Wells" submission may include both factual and legal arguments designed to bolster the defendant's case. When making factual arguments, one should keep in mind that the SEC may have access to documents not within the possession of the defendant and, therefore, one should try to limit the arguments to ones that can be supported and substantiated by a tangible document or testimony. With legal arguments, one has a little more leeway, and citing case law can be appropriate to bring forth legal positions to the SEC's attention. One should also consider including potential extenuating circumstances that can be explained to the SEC, which may put the defendant in a more sympathetic light or evidence of remedial actions that the defendant may have taken. It is also important to keep in mind that the audience for the "Wells" submission is both the Enforcement staff and the Commissioners and their counsel who may not be as knowledgeable about the facts of the matter.

In most instances, it is not helpful to allege wrongdoing on the part of SEC Enforcement staff in the "Wells" submission as unless extremely blatant and easily provable, such allegations will not be accepted by the SEC.

Bondi explains that when it comes to "Wells" submissions, the most important thing is to understand who your audience is and notes that this may not always be the same answer for every case. For instance, Bondi explains that one may wish to write a submission that is very strong and geared toward the Commissioners and their counsel. In other instances, one may want to gear the submission more towards the Enforcement. Alternatively, one may wish to gear it toward both audiences. Bondi explains that the key to the "Wells" submission is credibility, specifying that whenever one puts any information in the submission, one must be able to source that information. Bondi notes that one cannot make a statement that is not supported by some sort of document or evidence; otherwise, it becomes simply conjecture. In addition, Bondi stresses that one should not oversell a position, whether it involves the facts or the law.

Bondi further advises defendants to pick battles wisely in a "Wells" submission. He explains that there may be points where the defendant may have had a lapse or made a legitimate mistake, and fighting every single battle, including ones where the defendant is clearly at fault, will reduce the credibility of the entire submission.

He also explains that one must frame the issues well, noting that in litigation, he has always found that the party that frames the issues the best wins the argument. He stresses that framing the issues to the SEC and understanding, in particular, that the SEC Commissioner and their counsel are extremely busy and are likely receiving this "Wells" submission for the first time. Bondi notes that these SEC Commissioners have not been living with the facts like the defendants and their counsel and Enforcement staff have been. For this reason, Bondi recommends that defendants keep the submission simple and make it easy for the reader to understand and cut right to the crux of the issues. Bondi notes that as an advisor to SEC Commissioners, he used to read more than 50 "Wells" submissions in a month. Bondi recalls how some of the "Wells" submissions he reviewed while at the SEC were incredibly complicated and hard to read to the extent that when he finished reading some of them, he would scratch his head and say, "OK, I have no idea what arguments this person was trying to make." Bondi states that in his view, the biggest fault he sees in "Wells" submissions is that defendants try to pack a great deal of information into the submission and presuppose that the reader has a strong background in the matter.

A "Wells" meeting may also be helpful for defendants to have the opportunity to make their case face-to-face to the SEC. Defendants may request multiple meetings with various levels of SEC staff and may wish to consider if escalating the matter to a more senior-level Enforcement official makes sense. These instances often occur in high-profile matters and as a general matter, the senior-level officials back up the Enforcement staff, but there is always the possibility that a new actor may respond to defendants' arguments differently.

7.7 USE OF EXPERTS IN SEC ENFORCEMENT PROCEEDINGS

Bondi also recommends that defendants consider using experts at various stages of the Enforcement proceeding to buttress their defense efforts. Bondi noted that experts are particularly important when it comes to complicated questions of accounting, indicating that if there is a question about an accounting judgment, experts may play a particularly valuable role. He also suggested that market structure-type experts can be helpful as well. Bondi explains that there are really two types of experts: (1) an expert that is being used to assist in an internal investigation, either for management or for the audit committee; and (2) an expert whom the defendant would engage to advocate and submit an expert report that you might wish to attach to a "Wells" submission or submit to the court. Bondi stated that he would not normally bring the expert who would submit an expert report on behalf of the defendant to the actual "Wells" meeting, but rather let the expert speak through the report provided as part of the "Wells" submission. He explained that there is no great up-side to bringing the expert to the "Wells" meeting, but it does have the potential down-side of giving the SEC Enforcement staff a free opportunity to cross-examine the expert.

I have served as an expert in SEC proceedings and know first-hand how useful expert testimony can be to the defendant's case. Often, arguments made by legal counsel, even if well-constructed and argued, can be viewed by judges or juries as lacking credibility because the source of the arguments is the attorneys paid to represent the defendant. If a defendant can find a respected expert in the field who can supplement legal arguments with expert opinions that are advantageous to the defendant's cause, the defendant's positions become much more persuasive and credible and can often make the difference in prevailing in court or in discussions with the SEC.

7.8 SETTLEMENT DISCUSSIONS

Most of the SEC Enforcement cases are resolved through a settlement rather than the matter going to trial. Settlement discussions often commence during the "Wells" process. For the most part, settlements are not admissible as evidence of wrongdoing, particularly where the settlement includes language that the defendant is not admitting any allegations or liability. In recent years, the SEC has moved to attempt to require defendants to admit liability in certain matters, which will complicate the decision of a defendant to agree to a settlement. The advantage of a settlement is that it resolves the matter for publicity purposes and the costs of litigating can be very high. Often settlement discussions will surround the particular charge that the defendant will be found to have violated, as defendants will try to avoid a fraud charge, which has collateral consequences.

Bondi explains that it is a judgment call dependent on the facts of a particular case when and how to raise settlement with the SEC. He also notes that it is dependent upon whom one is dealing with at the SEC, explaining that certain SEC staff members view the raising of a settlement issue with them too early as "blood in the water." Bondi does say that one thing that is clear is that one cannot raise settlement discussions while the SEC Enforcement staff are in the middle of their investigation. Settlement discussions cannot be initiated in the middle of testimony or while the defendant is producing documents in response to a subpoena, according to Bondi, as that would be met with skepticism and distrust. But if it appears as though the SEC staff is finished with their investigation, and open to reaching a settlement, Bondi says that one may consider proactively saying to the staff that there is an interest in having potential settlement discussions.

7.9 TRENDS IN SEC ENFORCEMENT

Companies should also be aware of several recent trends in SEC Enforcement in order to properly defend themselves in these proceedings. Bondi points to the increased use by the SEC of administrative proceedings, rather than bringing an action in federal court.

The Dodd-Frank Act amended the Securities Act to allow the SEC to impose civil money penalties against non-regulated persons or entities in administrative proceedings before an administrative law judge. While the SEC has always used administrative proceedings, since the enactment of the Dodd-Frank Act, the SEC has begun utilizing administrative proceedings for a much larger number of cases, including insider trading cases that had previously been brought before a federal court. Some believe that the SEC's increased use of administrative proceedings relates to some of the objections they have received from federal judges in recent years to settlements they have attempted to enter into with defendants.[5]

Some of the key differences between proceedings brought in the administrative arena and those brought in federal court are that administrative proceedings have limited discovery – they do not require a jury trial and administrative proceedings are governed by SEC rules, not Federal Rules of Civil Procedure. The other significant difference is that the administrative law judge who is deciding the case is an employee of the SEC, rather than a federal judge who has no alliances to any party. Even though the administrative law judge acts independently of the rest of the SEC, this individual is still an SEC employee. Bondi notes that in administrative proceedings, discovery is very curtailed for defendants. Accordingly, if one has a big, witness-intense case that appears to be heading to an administrative proceeding, Bondi advises that counsel for a defendant needs to conduct "self-discovery" very quickly. Bondi explains that unlike federal court where there is a significant amount of discovery, including depositions and ample time to learn the facts of the case, in an administrative proceeding, discovery is very curtailed and there are very tight time frames. Thus, according to Bondi, one needs to be proactive to begin building a factual record by reaching out both to internal and external witnesses as soon as possible to get up to speed on the case. It is worth noting that, prior to instituting the administrative proceeding, the SEC has had as much time as it needs, often several years, to subpoena information and testimony to build its factual record and therefore limited discovery and tight deadlines in an administrative proceeding are distinct advantages for the government.

Bondi also points to the revamped SEC whistleblower program as representing increased incentives for individuals to come forward with complaints and allegations. Bondi foresees that many new whistleblowers will be attracted by the recent large awards granted

---

[5]One of the most publicized rejections of an SEC settlement by a federal court was a September 2011 refusal by Judge Jed Rakoff of the U.S. District Court for the Southern District of New York to approve a proposed SEC settlement with Citibank wherein Citibank would pay $285 million to settle charges about misleading investors in relation to the housing market. See Judge Rakoff opinion at http://rrbdlaw.com/images/RakoffSECCiti.pdf.

by the SEC, and this will significantly impact companies in the next several years.

Finally, Bondi noted the SEC Enforcement staff's newly aggressive use of "admissions" as referenced above. Bondi explains that, from the earliest days of the SEC enforcement initiative, the norm was to allow companies to settle without admitting or denying fault. This norm was important, according to Bondi, as it allowed companies to resolve matters with the SEC without having to worry about collateral consequences of having their admissions used in civil litigation and other parallel proceedings such as criminal proceedings. However, in June of 2013, SEC Chair Mary Jo White announced a shift in SEC Enforcement policy that the SEC would begin to require defendants to admit to liability for their conduct in the following situations: (1) misconduct that harmed large numbers of investors, or placed investors or the market at risk of potentially serious harm, (2) egregious intentional misconduct, or (3) when the defendant engaged in unlawful obstruction of the Commission's investigative processes. Previous to this new policy, the SEC had required admissions only in cases where a defendant pleads guilty in a parallel criminal proceeding or enters a deferred prosecution or non-prosecution agreement.

Bondi explains that the new SEC Enforcement policy on admissions is significant on two fronts. First, according to Bondi, it makes it more difficult for some companies to settle particularly where an admission may have a collateral consequence. With defense contractors, for example, an admission of fraud would result in their debarment from any future governmental contracts. Secondly, Bondi has seen how admissions can be used either intentionally or unintentionally as leverage for the SEC Enforcement staff to obtain larger penalties in a negotiated settlement to a proceeding. Bondi explains that, if defendants are fearful that the SEC Enforcement staff may seek an admission, companies may be willing to settle for greater amounts. Bondi says that the SEC Enforcement staff sometimes would say the following at the beginning of settlement negotiations, "We are open to resolving the case. We have not determined whether we will seek an admission or not. We are considering recommending that we seek an admission but we are hoping to settle it now, how much are you willing to pay?" The implication, according to Bondi, is that if the defendant is willing to pay a large penalty as settlement, the SEC will not seek an admission.

Partially as a result of criticism of a lack of aggressiveness in bringing actions against those who may have contributed to the financial crisis, and its high-profile failures to uncover frauds like Bernie Madoff's $50 billion Ponzi scheme, the SEC Enforcement Division has in recent years begun utilizing new tools such as administrative proceedings and requiring admissions to increase its leverage against defendants and be more aggressive in its efforts to pursue alleged violators of the securities laws. Defending these cases has become more challenging as a result. Companies, therefore, need to be proactive when they first learn of the SEC Enforcement Division conducting an investigation. They need to conduct their own internal investigations so that they have as many facts as possible about what the government will be looking at as a basis for potential action.

If the SEC seeks discovery, whether informal or formal, the company should cooperate but be sure to allow sufficient time to prepare their witnesses appropriately. Companies should take the necessary steps and time to review, assess, and organize documents being produced to the SEC so that they are fully aware of the consequences of what is being handed over to the government. Defendants should try to aggressively and intelligently use the "Wells" process to advance their defense. They should consider the audience for their presentations, retain experienced SEC counsel, preferably ones who are familiar with the SEC Enforcement staff attorneys handling the particular case, and utilize the assistance of experts as appropriate. If a formal action is approved, defendants should pursue both settlement options and aggressively prepare for trial. If the matter is brought in court before a jury, an expert can be useful to simplify the facts so that the jurors can understand why the government's position is not necessarily accurate. If the matter is brought before an administrative law judge, an expert can be utilized in a more sophisticated manner, as the administrative law judge will have significant experience with securities-related matters, and the expert has the ability to assert a more complex view of the defendant's position.

7.10 MINIMIZING EXPOSURE IN AN SEC ENFORCEMENT CASE

When a company is faced with an SEC Enforcement action, the consequences can be severe and frightening. The matters at issue can be very complex and small nuances may determine whether the company prevails at trial. Different approaches should be utilized depending upon whether the matter is brought before a federal court or an administrative law judge. Defending these proceedings can be extremely costly and there will likely be opportunities for settlement. Companies should weigh carefully the risks of turning down a possible settlement in favor of proceeding to trial.

When defending these types of actions more than any others, in my view, it is critical to retain knowledgeable counsel, with SEC experience, to litigate on behalf of the company. If the decision is made to go to trial, resources should be expended as necessary, including potentially hiring multiple experts to testify, to ensure the best possible defense is put forth. The SEC Enforcement attorneys can be very aggressive and can have teams with multiple members working on a matter for years to prepare the case to go forward. If companies are assisted by an experienced team and have the resources and time to match the SEC's efforts and energy, they can significantly increase their chances of either prevailing outright or negotiating a favorable settlement.

CHAPTER 8

How to Defend FINRA Enforcement Actions

When a firm becomes a FINRA member, it agrees to abide by the rules and regulations of the securities industry, and agrees to be subject to FINRA's jurisdiction. Under FINRA Rules, firms and associated persons are obligated to cooperate with FINRA staff when it conducts investigations. FINRA Rule 8210 requires FINRA's members, persons associated with its members, and any other person subject to FINRA's jurisdiction to provide information orally, in writing, or electronically as requested by FINRA and to testify at a location specified by FINRA staff, under oath or affirmation administered by a court reporter or a notary public if requested, with respect to any matter involved in a FINRA investigation, complaint, examination or proceeding.[1] Rule 8210 also allows FINRA staff to inspect and copy the books, records, and accounts of FINRA members.

FINRA's disciplinary actions involving its members and associated persons charged with violations of FINRA Rules and the federal securities laws are resolved by disciplinary hearing proceedings.[2] The disciplinary process begins with the filing of a complaint with FINRA's Office of Hearing Officers.

Separate from the disciplinary process, aggrieved investors may bring claims against FINRA members through FINRA's arbitration

---

[1] See full text of FINRA Rule 8210 at http://finra.complinet.com/en/display/display_main .html?rbid=2403&element_id=3883.
[2] See ibid.

process. If an investor prevails in an arbitration against a FINRA member, the firm will be forced to pay the investor damages. Nearly all claims by investors against brokers are resolved through FINRA arbitration because FINRA requires customer/broker contracts to contain a "mandatory arbitration clause."[3]

8.1 FINRA DISCIPLINARY ACTIONS

In 2014, FINRA brought 1,397 disciplinary actions against registered individuals and firms, which levied more than $134 million in fines.[4] FINRA also referred more than 700 fraud and insider trading cases to the SEC and other Agencies for litigation and/or prosecution in 2014.[5]

Richard A. Roth, founder and partner of the Roth Law Firm, and a recognized expert in FINRA Enforcement proceedings, also serves as an arbitrator for FINRA. He is well known for his extensive litigation and arbitration successes and the numerous litigation awards and verdicts he has received over the years. He states that there are a wide variety of different actions that FINRA brings. Roth provides some recent examples of disciplinary proceedings brought by FINRA, as follows: (1) complaints against brokers for violating FINRA Rule 3270, which requires each registered representative of a broker-dealer to provide the broker-dealer with annual prior written notice of all outside business activities; (2) claims that brokers conducted trades with customers away from their employing firm, in what is known as "trading away"; and (3) customer arbitration issues, such as suitability (where FINRA challenges the suitability of recommendations made to retail investors for complex products), churning (where a broker or financial advisor excessively buys and sells a client's securities to increase their own commissions), and/or breach of fiduciary duty by brokers vis-à-vis their customers.

A review of the FINRA public disciplinary actions database reveals the following additional areas in which FINRA has, in the

---

[3]For more detailed information about FINRA's arbitration process see the website at http://www.finra.org/ArbitrationAndMediation/index.htm.
[4]See http://www.finra.org/AboutFINRA/WhatWeDo/.
[5]See https://www.finra.org/AboutFINRA/.

past few years, instituted disciplinary actions through enforcement proceedings:

- **Residential Mortgage-Backed Securities ("RMBS") and Commercial Mortgage-Backed Securities ("CMBS").** FINRA has brought actions regarding disclosure requirements for issuers of subprime RMBS of historical performance information for past securitizations that contain mortgage loans similar to those in the RMBS being offered to investors. For example, FINRA fined Citigroup Global Markets, Inc. $3.5 million for providing inaccurate mortgage performance information, supervisory failures, and other violations in connection with subprime RMBS.[6]
- **Collateralized Mortgage Obligations ("CMOs") and Collateralized Debt Obligations ("CDOs").** FINRA has brought several actions against firms for fraudulent sales of CMOs and CDOs and failure of supervision in this area. Specifically, a FINRA hearing panel ruled that Brookstone Securities, and the firm's owner/CEO and one of the firm's brokers, made fraudulent sales of CMOs to unsophisticated, elderly, and retired investors. FINRA fined Brookstone $1 million and ordered it to pay restitution of more than $1.6 million to customers. FINRA also barred Brookstone's owner and broker from the securities industry, and barred Brookstone's former CCO from acting in any supervisory or principal capacity, suspended him in all capacities for two years, and fined him $25,000.[7] FINRA also fined Guggenheim securities, LLC $800,000 for failing to supervise two CDO traders who engaged in activities to hide a trading loss and sanctioned the two traders.[8]
- **Non-Traded Real Estate Investment Trusts ("REITs").** FINRA issued an Investor Alert called *Public Non-Traded REITs – Perform a Careful Review Before Investing*[9] and after an

---

[6]See http://www.finra.org/Newsroom/NewsReleases/2012/P126482.

[7]See http://www.finra.org/Newsroom/NewsReleases/2012/P126718.

[8]See http://www.finra.org/Newsroom/NewsReleases/2012/P187302.

[9]See http://www.finra.org/Newsroom/NewsReleases/2011/P124582.

Enforcement proceeding, FINRA ordered David Lerner Associates, Inc. to pay approximately $12 million in restitution to affected customers who purchased shares in Apple REIT Ten, a non-traded $2 billion REIT that DLA sold and to customers who were charged excessive markups.[10]

* **Exchange-Traded Products ("ETPs").** FINRA brought several proceedings against firms in connection with selling leveraged and inverse Exchange-Traded Funds ("ETFs") including an action against Citigroup Global Markets, Inc.; Morgan Stanley & Co., LLC; UBS Financial Services; and Wells Fargo Advisors, LLC, assessing a total of more than $9.1 million in fines for selling leveraged and inverse ETFs without reasonable supervision and for not having a reasonable basis for recommending the securities. The firms were fined more than $7.3 million and required to pay a total of $1.8 million in restitution to certain customers who made unsuitable leveraged and inverse ETF purchases.[11] FINRA also ordered J.P. Turner & Co., L.L.C. to pay $707,559 in restitution to 84 customers for sales of unsuitable leveraged and inverse ETFs and for excessive mutual fund switches.[12] FINRA also brought Enforcement actions against two additional companies and issued significant fines and ordered restitution payments to customers in connection with sales of leveraged and inverse ETFs and failure to supervise the sale of non-traded REITs.[13]

* **Over-concentration in complex products.** FINRA issued fines and ordered restitution against a number of firms for matters related to the sales of complex products, primarily focusing on failure of supervision. For example, FINRA fined LPL Financial LLC $950,000 for supervisory deficiencies related to the sales of alternative investment products, oil and gas partnerships, business development companies ("BDCs"), hedge funds, managed

---

[10]See http://www.finra.org/Newsroom/NewsReleases/2011/P123738.

[11]See http://www.finra.org/Newsroom/NewsReleases/2012/P126123.

[12]See http://www.finra.org/Newsroom/NewsReleases/2013/P397504.

[13]See http://www.finra.org/Newsroom/NewsReleases/2014/P412654 and http://www.finra.org/Newsroom/NewsReleases/2014/P448889.

futures, and other illiquid pass-through investments.[14] FINRA also fined Wells Fargo and Banc of America a total of $2.15 million and ordered the firms to pay more than $3 million in restitution to customers for losses incurred from unsuitable sales of floating-rate bank loan funds.[15] FINRA fined Morgan Stanley $600,000 for failing to have a reasonable supervisory system and procedures in place to notify supervisors whether structured product purchases complied with the firm's internal guidelines related to concentration (the size of an investment in relation to the customer's liquid net worth) and minimum net worth[16] and Merrill Lynch $1,000,000 for failing to have a reasonable supervisory system that would flag for supervisors on an automated exception basis potentially unsuitable concentration levels in structured products in customer accounts.[17]

- **AML compliance.** FINRA's Enforcement department has long focused on actions brought against firms for failures of AML compliance, particularly as related to penny stock compliance. For example, FINRA fined Brown Brothers Harriman & Co. $8 million for substantial anti-money laundering compliance failures including, among other related violations, its failure to have an adequate anti-money laundering program in place to monitor and detect suspicious penny stock transactions;[18] FINRA fined COR Clearing $1 million for numerous failures to comply with AML, financial reporting, and supervisory obligations;[19] FINRA fined Oppenheimer and Co., Inc. $1,425,000 for the sale of unregistered penny stock shares and for failing to have an AML compliance program to detect and report suspicious penny stock transactions;[20] and FINRA fined Atlas One Financial, Firstrade Securities, and World Trade Financial Corp. $900,000 for failing to establish and implement adequate AML programs and other

---

[14] See http://www.finra.org/Newsroom/NewsReleases/2014/P468052.

[15] See http://www.finra.org/Newsroom/NewsReleases/2013/P269883.

[16] See http://disciplinaryactions.finra.org/Search/ViewDocument/27988.

[17] See http://www.finra.org/Newsroom/NewsReleases/2013/P242318.

[18] See http://www.finra.org/Newsroom/NewsReleases/2014/P443442.

[19] See http://www.finra.org/Newsroom/NewsReleases/2013/P408614.

[20] See http://www.finra.org/Newsroom/NewsReleases/2013/P314981.

supervisory systems to detect suspicious transactions. FINRA also fined and suspended four executives involved.[21]

- **Arbitration-related matters.** FINRA has brought proceedings against firms who restricted rights of customers, including a complaint against Charles Schwab & Company charging the firm with violating FINRA Rules by requiring its customers to waive their rights to bring class actions against the firm;[22] an action against Merrill Lynch that resulted in a $1 million fine and findings that Merrill Lynch failed to arbitrate disputes with employees relating to retention bonuses.[23]

- **Insider trading.** FINRA has brought actions for improper sharing of material non-public information, including an action against a Vice President at J.P. Morgan Securities, LLC, and a former registered representative at Meyers Associates, L.P., that resulted in them both being barred from the securities industry for their improper sharing of information regarding at least 15 pending corporate merger and acquisition transactions,[24] and for disclosure failures and lack of supervision in connection with potential insider trading, such as the action against Citigroup Global Markets that culminated in a $725,000 fine and findings that Citigroup failed to disclose certain conflicts of interest in its research reports and research analysts' public appearances[25] and the proceeding against Goldman Sachs which led to a $22 million fine for failing to supervise equity research analyst communications with traders and clients and for failing to adequately monitor trading in advance of published research changes to detect and prevent possible information breaches by its research analysts.[26]

- **Municipal securities.** FINRA has brought several proceedings arising out of fees paid from the proceeds of municipal and state bond offerings. For example, FINRA fined Citigroup, Goldman Sachs, JP Morgan, Merrill Lynch, and Morgan Stanley a total of

---

[21] See http://www.finra.org/Newsroom/NewsReleases/2013/P256514.
[22] See http://www.finra.org/Newsroom/NewsReleases/2012/P125517.
[23] See http://www.finra.org/Newsroom/NewsReleases/2012/P125455.
[24] See http://www.finra.org/Newsroom/NewsReleases/2014/P412652.
[25] See http://www.finra.org/Newsroom/NewsReleases/2012/P125369.
[26] See http://www.finra.org/Newsroom/NewsReleases/2012/P125974.

more than $4.48 million for payments they made to the California Public Securities Association, a group that conducts lobbying, requesting that those payments be reimbursed as underwriting expenses from the proceeds of the negotiated municipal and state bond offerings. FINRA also brought charges for inadequate disclosure of the nature of the fees to issuers, and the failure to have adequate systems and written supervisory procedures reasonably designed to monitor how the municipal securities associations used the funds that these firms paid.[27]

- **Excessive markups and markdowns.** FINRA has brought several actions against investment firms for charging excessive markups and markdowns in corporate bond transactions, including an action against StateTrust Investments, Inc. for charging excessive markups/markdowns to customers in a total of 563 transactions, which culminated in a $1.045 million fine and a six-month suspension of sanction against the firm's head trader.[28] In addition, FINRA fined Citi International $600,000 and ordered more than $648,000 in restitution and interest to more than 3,600 customers for charging excessive markups and markdowns on corporate and Agency bond transactions and for related supervisory violations.[29]

- **E-mail retention.** FINRA has instituted several Enforcement proceedings against firms for failure to preserve business-related e-mails. These actions have included a proceeding that culminated in a fine against Barclays Capital Inc. of $3.75 million for systemic failures to preserve electronic records and certain e-mails and instant messages in the manner required for a period of at least 10 years;[30] a $7.5 million fine against LPL Financial LLC for 35 separate, significant e-mail system failures, and for material misstatements made to FINRA during its investigation of the firm's e-mail failures,[31] and a $1.2 million fine issued

---

[27] See http://www.finra.org/Newsroom/NewsReleases/2012/P197554.
[28] See http://www.finra.org/Newsroom/NewsReleases/2013/P288973.
[29] See https://www.finra.org/Newsroom/NewsReleases/2012/P125821.
[30] See http://www.finra.org/Newsroom/NewsReleases/2013/P412646.
[31] See http://www.finra.org/Newsroom/NewsReleases/2013/P264524.

against five affiliates of ING for failing to retain or review millions of e-mails for periods ranging from two months to more than six years.[32]

- **Inadequate supervisory systems.** FINRA has brought actions against firms for various consequences of having inadequate supervisory systems, such as the proceeding that led to a $2.8 million fine against Merrill Lynch for supervisory failures that resulted in overcharging customers $32 million in unwarranted fees,[33] and for failing to provide certain required trade notices, and fines against five other firms (LPL Financial, LLC: $400,000 fine; Scottrade, Inc.: $50,000 fine; State Farm VP Management Corp.: $155,000 fine; T. Rowe Price, Inc.: $40,000 fine, and Deutsche Bank Securities, Inc.: $125,000 fine), for their failure to establish, maintain, and enforce reasonable supervisory systems and procedures to ensure timely mutual fund prospectus delivery.[34]

- **Books and records violations.** FINRA has brought cases for errors and a lack of transparency in firms' books and records. For example, FINRA brought an Enforcement proceeding against Deutsche Bank Securities, Inc. after an examination revealed that the firm's books reflected that it owed $9.4 billion to its affiliate, but neither the firm nor FINRA examiners could readily determine which portions of that debt were attributable to the customers' enhanced lending activity, and which were attributable to Deutsche Bank's own proprietary trading. FINRA also found that there were instances where the firm made inaccurate calculations that resulted in it overstating its capital or failing to set aside enough funds in its customer reserve account to appropriately protect customer securities. Eventually, Deutsche Bank Securities agreed to a $6.5 million fine.[35]

- **Cyber security.** FINRA has issued fines to companies in connection with cases brought arising out of customer breaches.

---

[32] See http://www.finra.org/Newsroom/NewsReleases/2013/P207604.

[33] See http://www.finra.org/Newsroom/NewsReleases/2012/P127129.

[34] See http://www.investorprotection.com/blog/2013/01/04/lpl-financial-fined-over-mutual-fund-issues/.

[35] See http://www.finra.org/Newsroom/NewsReleases/2013/P411637.

For example, Morgan Keegan was fined $150,000 for its failure to provide sufficient safeguards to detect, monitor for, and report customer data breaches, and its failure to provide adequate training to certain of its employees regarding customer breaches which resulted in firm employees failing to report customer data breaches timely to the firm.[36]

- **Regulation SHO**.[37] FINRA has brought proceedings against firms for violations relating to short selling and Regulation SHO, including a proceeding against Newedge USA, LLC for its failure to establish, maintain and enforce adequate supervisory systems and procedures that were reasonably designed to achieve compliance with Regulation SHO and for accepting customers' short sale orders without a reasonable basis to believe that the securities could be borrowed.[38]

8.2   FINRA ENFORCEMENT PROCESS

Roth explains that FINRA Enforcement actions can be triggered in three ways: (1) a referral from a FINRA exam; (2) a complaint by a whistleblower; and (3) where an arbitration has been commenced and FINRA decides to bring its own independent enforcement action.

Roth describes how the FINRA Enforcement process is initiated. He explains that FINRA enforcement staff will contact the broker or brokerage firm and ordinarily request documents and inform them that they are conducting an investigation. At first, FINRA will request records from the registered representative and his firm pursuant to FINRA Rule 8210. FINRA may also seek an "on-the-record" interview or "OTR" where FINRA representatives will ask the broker questions about the matter at issue under oath at a FINRA office. Broker or firm representatives should be aware that the information provided to FINRA may be used in a FINRA disciplinary proceeding, and may be shared with other regulatory Agencies, such as the

---

[36] See http://www.thinkadvisor.com/2012/06/21/sec-finra-dol-enforcement-roundup-investment-advic.

[37] The SEC adopted Regulation SHO in September 2004 to establish rules concerning short sale practices. See http://www.gpo.gov/fdsys/pkg/FR-2004-08-06/html/04-17571.htm.

[38] See http://www.finra.org/Newsroom/NewsReleases/2013/P299086.

SEC, and it may also be subpoenaed by others, including by customers' lawyers in arbitration proceedings, as well as shared with criminal investigators and prosecutors like the Justice Department and the FBI.

After the review of documents and interview, FINRA will conduct an analysis of the case, according to Roth, and make a determination as to whether it wishes to institute an Enforcement proceeding. If FINRA decides to go forward, as with the SEC Enforcement process, Roth explains that FINRA issues a "Wells Notice," which informs the defendant that FINRA intends to commence an Enforcement proceeding and describes the alleged improper action taken and the specific rules that FINRA is claiming were violated. The defendant then has the opportunity to submit a "Wells" submission to attempt to convince FINRA not to go forward with the Enforcement action.[39]

Roth says that the mistake some brokers make is that they do not engage counsel early enough in the FINRA Enforcement process. Roth explains that counsel should be retained as soon as the firm or broker is advised by FINRA staff that an investigation has been commenced. Roth says that many brokers retain counsel after they have produced documents to FINRA or after they have given an OTR. In this situation, Roth explains that once the defendant has given sworn testimony, the representation becomes more difficult, as the broker has already provided sworn testimony to FINRA. Roth advises that, even if the broker or firm does not believe it did anything wrong, it should not sit for an OTR with FINRA without retaining counsel and walking in prepared for the OTR, as this on-the-record interview is a pivotal moment in the case.

Roth also counsels that defendants should be aggressive in their "Wells" submissions to FINRA and should cite as appropriate to the OTR testimony to the extent the defendant does not feel as if FINRA has interpreted or quoted the testimony accurately. He gave an example where, after he submitted a "Wells" submission to FINRA citing the defendant's testimony, FINRA responded to his

---

[39] As explained in Chapter 7, the "Wells" notice and "Wells" submission are named after John Wells, the former SEC Committee Chair who first pioneered the process in the SEC.

client, saying, "You are right; we are not going forward with the case." Roth explains that the central point that defendants should be making in their "Wells" submissions is that FINRA is going to lose at trial and therefore the case is not worth pursuing.

FINRA may initiate an action or refer the matter to the SEC, which also has authority to directly enforce a FINRA Rule if FINRA chooses not to do so. The SEC does not consider its administrative proceedings duplicative of FINRA enforcement actions and may bring a separate action alongside the FINRA action.[40]

8.3 FINRA'S FORMAL PROCEEDING

FINRA's formal proceeding will be initiated with a complaint, to which the defendant has 25 days to answer. In the answer, defendants may and should request a hearing.

In terms of discovery, Roth explains that FINRA will ordinarily advise the defendant that he or she may view all documents in FINRA's files relating to the Enforcement action. Roth likens it to the obligation of a prosecutor to produce all documents to the defendant that they relied upon in bringing the case. In addition, the on-the-record interview generally conducted in the informal stage of the proceeding is usually the only interview of the defendant in the case. One area of frustration for Roth is that prior to the "Wells" notice, while counsel can request a copy of the on-the-record interview, counsel is not provided with copies of the exhibits to the interview at that point in time. FINRA allows counsel to view the exhibits at FINRA's offices, according to Roth, but may not keep them until after the "Wells" process when the decision is made by FINRA to go forward with the Enforcement action.

8.4 CHALLENGES OF FINRA ENFORCEMENT PROCESS

Roth explains that one of the biggest challenges that defendants face in FINRA Enforcement proceedings is the limited time in which they

---

[40]See *Jones v. SEC,* 115 F.3d 1173, 1182 (4th Cir. 1997).

have to collect the evidence needed to defend themselves at the hearing. FINRA has as much time as it needs to compile its evidence, while defendants may have to scramble to develop a defense in a far shorter period of time. Roth advises, however, that it is worthwhile to attempt to contact witnesses identified by FINRA as he gave an example of an instance where FINRA identified six different customers who purportedly were wronged by his broker client; he contacted each one of them, obtained affidavits from all six individuals contradicting FINRA's position, and eventually prevailed at the appeal of the hearing for his clients.

8.5 CONDUCT OF THE FINRA HEARING

The hearing is conducted by a three-member panel, one of whom is a FINRA Hearing Officer and the other two are industry representatives. FINRA states that the Hearing Officers are entirely independent of FINRA's Department of Enforcement.[41] When a complaint is filed, FINRA's Chief Hearing Officer or Deputy Chief Hearing Officer assigns a Hearing Officer to the case. The Hearing Officer is responsible for overseeing the proceeding to ensure that it is conducted in a fair and efficient manner, and serves as Chair of the Hearing Panel.

In addition, any dispositive motions made by the defendant are decided by the FINRA hearing officer, and according to Roth, such motions are very unlikely to be granted. This circumstance takes place because by definition, from the Hearing Officer's perspective, as he works for FINRA, if he thought there was a possible issue for summary disposition, they likely would not have brought the case in the first instance. Roth states that it makes sense to file these types of motions anyway, even if the motion is expected to be denied, because he is informing the issuing panel that he intends to present at the hearing. In one instance, Roth made a motion prior to the hearing for summary disposition based upon a particular argument and the motion was denied. He made the same argument at the hearing but

---

[41] http://www.finra.org/web/groups/industry/@ip/@enf/@adj/documents/industry/p0067 46.pdf.

his argument was rejected again. He then made the same argument on appeal and prevailed and the entire proceeding was dismissed against his client.

Prior to the hearing, a pre-hearing conference is scheduled by the FINRA Hearing Officer. The conference is usually held by telephone, and the defendant and a representative of FINRA must participate in the conference. During the conference, the Hearing Officer will ask all parties to discuss the case, and will attempt to identify convenient dates and locations for the hearing. A hearing date and pre-hearing schedule will then be established. A list of witnesses and exhibits, and copies of the exhibits, must be produced to the Hearing Officer and FINRA prior to the hearing. The defendant will also receive a list of all of the Department's witnesses and exhibits, and copies of the exhibits, before the hearing.

In terms of the actual FINRA hearing, Roth explains that while it is serious, it is typically far less formal than a court proceeding. The parties generally make opening statements to the Panel. FINRA then offers its evidence, which may include the testimony of witnesses or documentary exhibits. When FINRA finishes its presentation, the defendant will present its side through testimony and documents. When the parties have finished offering evidence, they will usually be allowed to offer final arguments to the Panel. The rules of evidence are not strictly applied and Roth notes that there are times when FINRA's evidence will amount to rank hearsay. He also explains that FINRA generally has the upper hand in a hearing as they can present evidence of on-the-record interviews they conducted of third-party witnesses, sometimes when the witness did not have effective counsel representing him or her. Roth says that FINRA's case often relies almost exclusively upon the testimony of FINRA's investigator, perhaps customers who claimed they were wronged, and documentary evidence.

Roth has found the FINRA panel members to be relatively sophisticated and knowledgeable, and that they do try to give the defendant the benefit of the doubt. Moreover, because the defendant can prevail on a two to one vote, even if the FINRA Hearing Officer is predisposed to accept FINRA's evidence, the industry panel members are able to decide the case in favor of the defendant against the wishes of the FINRA employee.

Roth advises defendants to always retain counsel if they have a FINRA hearing. He also recommends, in the appropriate case, that defendants retain experts to buttress their case. FINRA may present experts as well, and in those instances, it is important for the defendant to have its own expert testifying at the hearing.

8.6 SETTLEMENT POSSIBILITIES

Roth says that FINRA also offers mediation for Enforcement proceedings where a settlement can be worked out between the parties prior to the hearing. Settlement discussions can also be had throughout the proceeding, but Roth notes that often FINRA will request a harsher penalty than the defendant is willing to agree to and the parties are unable to come to a resolution. There is also the possibility for settlement after the hearing is concluded prior to the decision being rendered particularly if one of the parties gets the impression that the panel members are not favorably disposed to their arguments.

In making arguments in mediation or settlement discussions, Roth advises to refer to the FINRA sanction guidelines, to determine what may be an acceptable offer. Roth explains that FINRA is often unwilling to deviate from the sanction guidelines since the final resolution between the parties is generally disclosed to the public and FINRA is often concerned about setting bad precedents for the future.

8.7 DISCIPLINARY SANCTIONS AVAILABLE TO FINRA

The types of sanctions available to FINRA include the following:

- Impose fines.
- Censure a member or associated person.
- Suspend the membership of a member or registration of an associated person.
- Expel or cancel the membership of a member, or revoke or cancel the registration of an associated person.

- Suspend or bar a member or associated person from association with all members.
- Impose other sanctions within its discretion as appropriate under the circumstances, including rescission, restitution, and/or disgorgement.
- Issue both permanent and temporary cease and desist orders.

Following the hearing, the Hearing Officer may require the parties to file proposed findings of fact and conclusions of law, and post-hearing briefs. All proposed findings of fact and factual assertions in post-hearing briefs must be supported by specific references to the record of the proceeding. Roth states that a decision is generally rendered within 30 to 45 days after the hearing.

8.8   RIGHT TO APPEAL DECISION OF HEARING PANEL

If the hearing panel members rule in favor of FINRA after the hearing, the defendant has a right to appeal to the National Adjudicatory Council ("NAC"). The NAC is made up of industry executives and law professors who look at the hearing record and the legal issues. An appellate brief is submitted and the defendant presents an oral argument to the panel. Roth says it is rare that the NAC will overturn FINRA, but it does happen, citing a case where it was determined at the hearing that a broker should be barred for life and after the appeal to the NAC, Roth convinced the NAC to wholly overturn the hearing panel's decision and ruled that the broker should have no penalty assessed against him whatsoever.

After a determination by the NAC, one has a right to appeal to the SEC and if that fails, to appeal to federal court. Roth notes obstacles to the success of these appeals are tough but not insurmountable, as they are looking at the same legal issues and factual record that had been reviewed by the NAC.

8.9   RECENT TRENDS IN FINRA ENFORCEMENT

Overall, Roth says one trend he has seen is that FINRA continues to focus its Enforcement efforts against the small brokers, who often have limited resources to fight back. FINRA, according to Roth, is more reluctant to bring cases against the larger investment banks that have the funds to present strong defenses. For that reason, it is important for the smaller entities to be well prepared for Enforcement hearings, with counsel if possible, so that they are not taken advantage of through a case brought without sufficient evidence.

8.10   MOUNTING AN AGGRESSIVE DEFENSE

In contrast to SEC Enforcement actions, FINRA proceedings generally have some informality, proceed at a quick pace, and are not necessarily so complex. Some smaller firms believe they can prevail without counsel and without much preparation. Firms should be wary of this approach. While defending a FINRA Enforcement proceeding will not require anywhere near the resources of defending an SEC Enforcement action, one should be careful not to take the FINRA proceedings lightly. There are significant consequences to being sanctioned by FINRA both practically and through the loss of reputation. If a firm retains experienced counsel who is familiar with the FINRA process and hearings, and puts forward a strong, aggressive, and credible defense with multiple witnesses, including experts as needed, they generally have a decent chance to prevail.

CHAPTER 9

How to Defend CFTC Enforcement Actions

The CFTC, through its Division of Enforcement, also investigates and prosecutes alleged violations of the CEA and CFTC regulations. The CEA makes it illegal to trade a contract for the purchase or sale of a commodity for future delivery – a "futures contract" – unless the contract is executed on a federally designated exchange. The Division of Enforcement bases investigations on information it develops independently, as well as information provided by other CFTC divisions; industry self-regulatory associations; state, federal, and international authorities; and members of the public. When the CFTC obtains evidence that criminal violations of the CEA have occurred, it may refer the matter to the Department of Justice for prosecution. Criminal activity involving commodity-related instruments can result in prosecution for criminal violations of the CEA and for violations of other federal criminal statutes, including commodities fraud, mail fraud, wire fraud, and conspiracy.

9.1 INCREASED AGGRESSIVENESS ON THE PART OF CFTC ENFORCEMENT

During the past several years, Congress has substantially expanded the CFTC's regulatory reach and the CFTC has become more aggressive in conducting enforcement. The CFTC has dramatically increased its annual enforcement action totals, and has imposed record high financial penalties on many market participants. In fiscal year 2014, the CFTC filed 67 new Enforcement actions and obtained a record $3.27 billion in monetary sanctions imposed against companies and individuals. The $3.27 billion in sanctions includes more than $1.8 billion in civil monetary penalties and more than $1.4 billion in restitution and disgorgement. These numbers bring the CFTC's total monetary sanctions over the past two fiscal years to more than $5 billion, which was more than the total sanctions imposed during the prior 10 fiscal years combined.[1]

Two of the primary reasons for the increased Enforcement actions are the expansion of the CFTC's Enforcement authority pursuant to the Dodd-Frank Act and the new CFTC whistleblower program. The Dodd-Frank Act impacted the CFTC Enforcement authority in a number of ways. Section 753 of the Dodd-Frank Act enhanced the CFTC's "anti-manipulation authority" to strengthen the CFTC's enforcement powers.[2] Pursuant to this section and CFTC implementing regulations, the CFTC is able to rely on evidence of "reckless" misconduct in addition to "specific intent" to prove manipulation. With this change, the CFTC can bring an action against "the reckless use of fraud-based manipulative schemes" without having to demonstrate that the defendant specifically intended to perpetrate the manipulative scheme. This change makes a significant difference in the level of proof needed to bring and prevail in an Enforcement action.

In addition, the Dodd-Frank Act expanded the CFTC's authority to bring new types of Enforcement actions alleging false statements to the CFTC. Prior to the Dodd-Frank Act, the CEA prohibited the dissemination of false information to the CFTC only in registration applications or CFTC-filed reports. However, the Dodd-Frank Act expanded this prohibition to also forbid the dissemination of false information through false statements of material fact made to the CFTC.

Further, section 747 of the Dodd-Frank Act amended the CEA to newly prohibit "disruptive practices," making it unlawful for

---

[1] See http://www.cftc.gov/PressRoom/PressReleases/pr7051-14.
[2] See section 6(c)(1) of the CEA.

market participants to: (1) violate bids or offers; (2) intentionally or recklessly disregard the orderly execution of transactions during the closing period; or (3) engage in spoofing.[3] Spoofing is bidding or offering with the intention to cancel the bid or offer before execution and under the CFTC's interpretation of this amendment, spoofing does not require evidence of a pattern of activity. The above changes, together with the new regulations promulgated pursuant to the Dodd-Frank Act regarding entities such as swap dealers, commodity pool operators and commodity trading advisors,[4] has and likely will continue to result in a substantially increased number of Enforcement actions.

In addition, the CFTC whistleblower program is already having an impact on CFTC Enforcement actions. The number of whistleblower claims filed with the CFTC jumped from 58 in fiscal year 2012 to 138 in fiscal 2013 to 227 in fiscal year 2014.[5] In May of 2014, the CFTC announced it would make its first whistleblower award of approximately $240,000 to an individual for providing valuable information about violations of the CEA.[6] The whistleblower program provides the CFTC with a new avenue to learn about potential violations of the CEA and has led and will lead to more Enforcement actions being commenced.

9.2 TYPES OF ENFORCEMENT ACTIONS BROUGHT BY THE CFTC

In attempting to understand CFTC's Enforcement priorities going forward, it is also helpful to analyze the types of Enforcement actions that the CFTC has brought in recent years. In 2014, for example, the CFTC Division of Enforcement focused its resources on the following areas:

[3] See section 4(c)(a)(5) of the CEA.
[4] See Chapter 6, for an in-depth discussion of the new entities subject to CFTC (and NFA) jurisdiction as a result of the Dodd-Frank Act.
[5] http://www.cftc.gov/ucm/groups/public/@whistleblowernotices/documents/file/wb_fy2014reporttocongress.pdf.
[6] http://www.cftc.gov/PressRoom/PressReleases/pr6933-14.

- **Commodity pool frauds.** The CFTC commenced several actions against alleged operators of fraudulent commodity pool schemes. For example, in late 2014, the CFTC brought an action against a non-registered individual, who, the CFTC claimed from January 2009 through March 2011, fraudulently solicited $1,146,000 from 43 pool participants to participate in pooled investment vehicles to trade in off-exchange agreements, contracts, or transactions in foreign currency (forex) on a leveraged or margined basis. The CFTC found that the defendant guaranteed monthly returns between 2 percent and 5 percent to pool participants who entered into six-month contracts, purportedly generating such returns by pooling participants' funds and trading in off-exchange forex transactions on a leveraged or margined basis. The CFTC ordered the defendant to pay a $700,000 civil monetary penalty and restitution of $766,625.30.[7] In 2014, the CFTC brought several additional actions regarding commodity pool schemes, charging several individuals with commodity pool fraud and obtaining judgments and settlements against several others.
- **Illegal precious metals transactions.** Another particular focus of the CFTC in 2014 was precious metals schemes and illegal precious metals transactions. The CFTC issued orders and brought actions against entities it determined were engaged in fraudulent precious metal schemes, including ordering a Florida-based company and individual to pay over $6.2 million in restitution and fines for soliciting individual retail customers to enter into financed precious metals transactions in gold, silver, and platinum but not actually purchasing physical commodities on the customers' behalf.[8] In addition, in 2014, the CFTC charged several individuals and companies with engaging in illegal precious metal transactions and obtained judgments against several others after trial, including obtaining over $5 million in restitution and penalties in early 2014 against two Florida residents and

---

[7]See http://www.cftc.gov/PressRoom/PressReleases/pr7091-14.
[8]See http://www.cftc.gov/PressRoom/PressReleases/pr6859-14.

their companies for improperly accepting orders and funds from customers of telemarketing firms for the purchase of physical precious metals on a leveraged basis.[9]

- **Manipulation cases.** In 2014, the CFTC also brought several actions arising out of alleged manipulation of foreign exchange benchmark interest rates, as well as manipulation and attempted manipulation of crude oil futures contracts and natural gas futures prices. In November 2014, the CFTC issued five Orders filing and settling charges against Citibank N.A., HSBC Bank plc, and JPMorgan Chase Bank N.A., The Royal Bank of Scotland plc and UBS AG for attempted manipulation of, and for aiding and abetting other banks' attempts to manipulate, global foreign exchange (FX) benchmark rates to benefit the positions of certain traders. The Orders collectively impose over $1.4 billion in civil monetary penalties.[10]

- **Ponzi schemes.** The CFTC continued its focus on Ponzi schemes in 2014, charging several individuals with conducting multi-million-dollar Ponzi schemes, including an action brought in September 2014 against an Ohio resident with soliciting at least $116 million from customers but only depositing $4.7 million of those funds into futures accounts.[11]

- **False statements to the CFTC.** The CFTC has been aggressive in bringing actions against those who they believe were not truthful with them in investigations. In 2014, the CFTC settled two cases against individuals who they claimed made false and misleading statements to them in the course of Enforcement investigations. In both cases, the CFTC obtained a penalty of $250,000. One matter involved a foreign national, who allegedly made false and misleading statements of material fact to CFTC staff in an interview during a CFTC Enforcement investigation, regarding a trade in Japanese Yen call options contracts[12] and the second one involved an individual who had provided CFTC

---

[9] See http://www.cftc.gov/PressRoom/PressReleases/pr6850-14.
[10] See http://www.cftc.gov/PressRoom/PressReleases/pr7056-14.
[11] See http://www.cftc.gov/PressRoom/PressReleases/pr7001-14.
[12] See http://www.cftc.gov/PressRoom/PressReleases/pr6815-14.

Enforcement staff with a signed and notarized financial disclosure statement in connection with the investigation in which he, according to the CFTC, falsely represented that the statement included all his known assets.[13]

- **Failure to file required reports.** In 2014, the CFTC also brought actions against firms for submitting inaccurate reports, settling with J.P. Morgan Chase and imposing a $650,000 civil penalty for one of its bank's subsidiaries submitting inaccurate reports about required reporting positions held by certain large traders;[14] and settling charges against two Brazil-based companies that produce and trade cotton and other agricultural products, for failing to comply with their legal obligation as reportable traders to submit weekly Form 304 Reports that show their call cotton purchases and sales.[15]
- **Supervision violations.** The CFTC also brought several actions in 2014 against firms for supervision violations, including actions against Deutsche Bank Securities,[16] Morgan Stanley Smith Barney,[17] and Merrill Lynch,[18] issuing significant fines and penalties.

The CFTC also focused heavily on several of these areas in 2013 and 2012 including commodity pool frauds, Ponzi schemes, and supervision cases. It is likely that CFTC Enforcement efforts will only increase in the next few years, with a particular emphasis on the areas where the CFTC increased its jurisdiction and authority pursuant to the Dodd-Frank Act. As CFTC investigations often take several years, individuals and companies will likely see an even greater increase in manipulation cases brought under the new "reckless" standard as well as actions for "disruptive practices" and "false statements" in the coming years.

---

[13] See http://www.cftc.gov/PressRoom/PressReleases/pr6880-14.

[14] See http://www.cftc.gov/PressRoom/PressReleases/pr6968-14.

[15] See http://www.cftc.gov/PressRoom/PressReleases/pr6827-14.

[16] See http://www.cftc.gov/PressRoom/PressReleases/pr7089-14.

[17] See http://www.cftc.gov/PressRoom/PressReleases/pr6998-14.

[18] See http://www.cftc.gov/PressRoom/PressReleases/pr6984-14.

9.3 TRIGGERS FOR CFTC ENFORCEMENT ACTIONS

According to Kenneth W. McCracken, a former Chief Trial Attorney in the CFTC's Division of Enforcement, and currently a partner at the law firm of Schiff Hardin LLP where he represents individuals and companies in investigations and litigations brought by the CFTC, and a recognized expert in CFTC Enforcement matters,[19] CFTC investigations are most commonly triggered by complaints from customers, market participants, whistleblowers, and referrals from other CFTC divisions and the NFA. McCracken says that the CFTC Divisions of Market Oversight and Swap Dealer and Intermediate Oversight may also refer matters to the Division of Enforcement based on what they have seen in their oversight activities and their analysis of the markets. In addition, referrals can come from state Agencies or other federal Agencies, such as the SEC or Federal Energy Regulatory Commission (FERC).

9.4 CFTC ENFORCEMENT PROCESS

McCracken explains that the Enforcement process at the CFTC often begins with an informal inquiry where the CFTC begins investigating matters even prior to seeking formal authority to issue a subpoena. The CFTC will then likely seek documents and information from companies or individuals. McCracken notes that the CFTC's initial document requests are often broad by design so they can gather the most information in order to better understand the issues they may be interested in. He also explains that the CFTC Enforcement staff is often agreeable to a rolling production of requested documents and will generally be understanding of smaller entities that might not be as technologically sophisticated and therefore may need more time to gather the documents the CFTC is seeking. McCracken says the CFTC, while open to limiting or tailoring the scope or breadth

---

[19] In over 10 years at the CFTC, Mr McCracken led or supervised teams of attorneys in the investigation and litigation of matters involving market manipulations, frauds, and trade practice violations and was a member of the Division of Enforcement's Manipulation and Disruptive Trading Squad.

of its requests, is not likely to do so unless it is convinced the original request will not reasonably result in obtaining the specific information it seeks.

In his experience while at the CFTC, McCracken found that many companies would cooperate with the CFTC when asked to voluntarily provide documents or information without a subpoena. In so doing, the CFTC could assume that these companies wish to build a sense of cooperation and trust with the regulatory Agency. In his experience while at the CFTC, he rarely encountered anyone that completely refused to abide by a CFTC voluntary request. McCracken notes that if a company refused to cooperate, its refusal would likely become an impetus for the Division of Enforcement to request subpoena authority from the CFTC Commission and issue a subpoena requesting the same information anyway. Accordingly, a company might delay the immediate need to respond to a CFTC voluntary document request, but may face a subpoena in the near future.

9.5 DIFFERENCES BETWEEN CFTC AND SEC ENFORCEMENT PROCEEDINGS

McCracken also notes that the CFTC Enforcement process functions differently than the SEC in that the CFTC Enforcement attorneys undertake both the investigation and the litigation of the matter. He explains that unlike at the SEC, there are not certain attorneys that investigate and then pass off the matter to litigating attorneys. In the CFTC process, the investigation is conducted by attorneys and investigators from the Division of Enforcement. In some matters, an economist may be added to the team, if there are complex economic issues that need to be understood. The Enforcement team would investigate the matter and, if necessary, subpoena or request voluntary documents and take investigative testimony. After review and analysis of all of the documents and information, according to McCracken, the Enforcement team would make a decision as to whether they believe there is a violation of the law. If they decide there is no violation, they would recommend closure of the case.

9.6 THE CFTC "WELLS" PROCESS

McCracken explains that if the CFTC Division of Enforcement decides to go forward with litigation, they must get approval from the Commission to file an Enforcement action. In addition, as is the case with the SEC, the CFTC utilizes a type of "Wells" process. According to McCracken, the CFTC "Wells" process may not necessarily be offered in every case, though it is still available. McCracken notes that in the more complex CFTC cases, such as alleged manipulations, the CFTC is more likely to offer the "Wells" process. He also explains, however, that even if not offered by the CFTC, a potential defendant can still request to submit a "Wells" or "white paper" or other legal document that argues and explains the potential defendant's positions prior to the CFTC approving an investigation for an Enforcement litigation action. If a potential defendant makes that request, McCracken believes that, more often than not, the Division of Enforcement likely will accept the submission and make it available to the Commission.

Where the "Wells" process is utilized, McCracken explains that the "Wells" submission would be submitted to the Division of Enforcement, and then as part of the normal internal process to request that a litigation action be formally brought, CFTC Enforcement would attach the "Wells" submission to its request for enforcement action that goes to the CFTC Commissioners. McCracken notes that it is the Division of Enforcement's prerogative as well to respond to whatever a potential defendant puts in the "Wells" submission in a memorandum that the Division of Enforcement will attach to its materials provided to the Commissioners.

The CFTC has set forth informal procedures that attempt to describe their "Wells" process. Under these procedures, the Division of Enforcement, in its discretion, may inform persons who may be named in a proposed enforcement proceeding of the nature of the allegations pertaining to them. Enforcement may then, in its discretion, advise such persons that they may submit a written statement prior to the consideration by the Commission of any staff recommendation for the commencement of such proceeding. These procedures specify that any written statements shall be submitted within

14 days after persons are informed by the Division of Enforcement of the nature of the proposed allegations pertaining to them and shall be no more than 20 pages, double spaced on $8\frac{1}{2}$ by 11 inch paper, setting forth their views of factual, legal, or policy matters relevant to the commencement of an Enforcement proceeding. The procedures also provide that any statement of fact included in the submission must be sworn to by a person with personal knowledge of such fact. The procedures also say that the Commission may, in its discretion, consider all, any portion, or none of the submission when it considers the staff recommendation to commence an Enforcement proceeding.[20]

McCracken explains that, in such cases, the CFTC Enforcement attorneys draft a complaint and provide it to the Commission together with a memorandum from Enforcement to the Commissioners requesting authority to file the complaint, any "Wells" submission from the potential defendant, and Enforcement's response to the "Wells" submission. At that point, the Commissioners would vote on whether Enforcement would have the authority to file the complaint. If the vote is affirmative, a complaint is filed and the formal litigation proceeding begins.

9.7 CFTC ENFORCEMENT'S USE OF EXPERTS

McCracken explains that in basic fraud matters, CFTC Enforcement likely will use its in-house investigators and economists for financial data analysis, but may look to outside experts for assistance in trading practice and manipulation cases. These experts may be retained, according to McCracken, by the CFTC during both the investigation stage to assist them in better understanding the financial and economic data and determining how strong a potential Enforcement action may be, and during litigation, where the experts can explain to the judge or jury the economic particulars of the CFTC's case. McCracken also says he has seen many instances where potential defendants have hired their own experts to evaluate the market or

---

[20] 17 C.F.R. § 11.1, Appendix A.

financial data and provide an analysis both prior to litigation and during litigation. McCracken notes that derivatives, commodities, and swaps markets are some of the most complex financial instruments that exist, and it can be beneficial for defendants to retain someone who can provide the business and economic context to potentially educate a trial judge or jury about these complex matters. Further, if a defendant retains an expert for market or economic analysis, it could prove beneficial to mitigate any potential charges or possible penalties during settlement discussions with the CFTC.

9.8 SETTLEMENT DISCUSSIONS

McCracken explains that there could be some specific instances where defendants would be advantaged by speaking to the CFTC about settlement early on in the process. Over the last few years, the Division of Enforcement has been more aggressive in its settlement negotiations. For example, the CFTC could make an offer to settle a case (i.e., demanding civil monetary penalties, restitution, trading bans, etc.) and state that the settlement offer will only increase as the matter continues through litigation and comes closer to a trial date. If this were to occur, broaching the topic of settlement early on could be beneficial to a defendant to better assess how the CFTC may view the strength of its case.

Additionally, he says that defendants should keep in mind that the CFTC is a small Agency with limited resources and it is likely cognizant of the budgetary costs of a potentially lengthy trial. Therefore, according to McCracken, while the CFTC will consider the strength and complexity of the case it is bringing, it will also likely consider the amount of internal resources a trial requires (i.e., numbers and hours of attorneys, investigators, experts, etc.) in its decision about settlement. The CFTC is also aware that defendants must assess these same considerations. Accordingly, some of the more complex CFTC cases which required fact-intensive litigation may end up being settled before a trial as both sides may find it beneficial to do so.

9.9   CFTC ENFORCEMENT'S USE OF ADMINISTRATIVE PROCEEDINGS

Another significant difference between the SEC and the CFTC Enforcement programs is that, unlike the SEC, according to McCracken, the CFTC has greatly decreased their use of administrative proceedings over the past few years. He notes that most of the administrative hearings that have been brought over the last few years by CFTC Enforcement were registration revocation actions. These hearings occur, for example, after an individual is sued by the CFTC for fraud and he or she was a registrant. After the fraud case is resolved, if there is a determination of liability, the CFTC can bring an administrative action to revoke the individual's registration. McCracken further notes that in 2012, the CFTC eliminated their two internal administrative law judge positions and now they use retired law judges or rely on judges from other federal Agencies.[21]

9.10   TRENDS IN CFTC ENFORCEMENT

In terms of CFTC Enforcement trends going forward, with all the post-Dodd-Frank new authorities, McCracken sees the CFTC scrutinizing new registrations and exemptions to registration created under the Dodd-Frank Act changes. He would encourage registrants to be particularly meticulous about maintaining required documentation. He also believes that the CFTC will focus heavily on potential manipulation and disruptive trading violations, including analyzing the market activity of algorithmic and high frequency traders. In general, McCracken says the CFTC will likely continue to emphasize bringing Enforcement actions on matters that specifically impact the integrity of the market.

McCracken also notes that from his time at the CFTC and now representing defendants in CFTC actions, he has been struck that

---

[21] Notwithstanding this trend over the past several years, in late 2014 the CFTC Enforcement Director indicated in an interview with the *Wall Street Journal* that the CFTC may utilize administrative process more often in the future because of budgetary constraints. See http://www.wsj.com/articles/cftc-turns-toward-administrative-judges-1415573398.

though the CFTC is a small Agency it has still brought many highly complex legal actions. He explains that many of the legal issues the CFTC deals with are not always black and white in terms of whether violations have occurred, but legal shades of gray. He explains that in many market trading cases, the interpretation of the law requires a facts-and-circumstances approach to determine if firms or individuals have committed a violation and are liable. Accordingly, McCracken suggests defendants should conduct their own legal analysis of their activities to determine both their exposure and the potential regulatory perspective of the CFTC on the matter at issue.

He also explains that due to the legal and economic complexity of the issues, if defendants do a good job presenting their arguments, they may have a good chance of prevailing before a judge because the underlying legal and economic issues are often not clear cut and can be reasonably seen in different ways. McCracken also explains that in the same vein, during the initial investigative stages, potential defendants may consider if it is beneficial to try to convince the CFTC that a legal action against them is not warranted by providing specific information to the CFTC that would explain the unique business or economic context or environment in which the potential defendant's decisions were made, which may be a persuasive argument to CFTC Enforcement staff. McCracken notes that, because there are many diverse types of commodities in futures markets with sometimes unique business motives and economic rationales particular to the business of a specific commodity, or group of commodities, it may require a detailed explanation to the CFTC Enforcement staff.

9.11 FLAWED ASSUMPTIONS ABOUT CFTC ENFORCEMENT PROCESS

McCracken has found that some defense attorneys may have the opinion that since they have prior experience dealing with the SEC, their experience will be similar in defending a CFTC Enforcement proceeding. However, McCracken says that the CFTC can be very different than the SEC, as it is a smaller Agency with staff that has experience with a specific and complex marketplace. Currently, the

CFTC Division of Enforcement has approximately 150 attorneys across four offices (Washington D.C., New York, Chicago, and Kansas City),[22] whereas SEC Enforcement has approximately 1,300 hundred attorneys across 12 offices around the country.[23] As such, the CFTC enforcement attorneys may deal with less internal bureaucracy and thereby have greater opportunity to discuss the more difficult legal issues and cases with a wider range of colleagues or supervisors, or more readily exchange impressions of specific defenses presented by defense attorneys. According to McCracken, if one assumes that he or she can deal with the CFTC Division of Enforcement in the exact same manner they have historically dealt with SEC Enforcement, they may not be as successful. He also believes that because of their smaller size and historical principles-based regulatory approach the CFTC Enforcement staff may have to be more practical and nimble when enforcing the CEA and regulations in a given case than the perhaps more proscriptive bright-line regulatory approach of many other federal Agencies.

For these reasons, trying to understand the regulatory motivations and intentions of the CFTC in a particular Enforcement action may be critical to achieving a successful resolution to the case.

9.12 STRATEGIES FOR CFTC ENFORCEMENT CASES

In this author's view, the approach to be utilized in defending a CFTC Enforcement proceeding should be very different than the approaches in defending either an SEC or FINRA action. There may be more opportunities at the outset of the case to have a robust dialogue with the CFTC investigative team regarding the specifics of the case, particularly if the defendant company believes that the basis of the CFTC's action is predicated on a misunderstanding of the facts or law. The specter of a settlement that both sides could

---

[22]See the CFTC's Fiscal Year 2015 President's Budget & Performance Plan at http://www.cftc.gov/ucm/groups/public/@newsroom/documents/file/cftcbudget2015.pdf.

[23]See the SEC's Fiscal Year 2015 Budget Request Tables at http://www.sec.gov/about/reports/sec-fy2015-budget-request-tables.pdf.

agree upon should be considered throughout the proceeding, even at the eve of trial. If the matter is taken all the way to trial, it may make sense to retain experts with a focus on explaining the complexities of the matter to the judge or jury. It is important to be aware of the limited Agency resources available to the CFTC, as compared to the SEC, for example. While this does not mean the CFTC can necessarily be outspent or outgunned at trial, it is an important factor to consider when attempting to develop an effective strategy in a CFTC Enforcement proceeding.

CHAPTER 10

How to Defend NFA Enforcement Actions

T he NFA, as the SRO for the futures industry, conducts much of its oversight in the form of periodic on-site examinations, as discussed in greater length in Chapter 6. The NFA also establishes and enforces rules and standards for customer protection, provides an arbitration forum for futures- and forex-related disputes, and conducts screening to determine fitness to become or remain an NFA member.

10.1 NFA DISCIPLINARY ACTIONS

In addition, the NFA Rules provide for two types of disciplinary actions – a complaint and a Member and/or Associate Responsibility Action ("MRA/ARA"). According to Ronald Hirst, the Associate General Counsel/Enforcement Coordinator for the NFA, a complaint is the most common type of disciplinary action taken at the NFA and is issued by the NFA's Business Conduct Committee ("BCC")[1] if they find reason to believe that an NFA requirement is being, has been, or is about to be violated and that the matter should be adjudicated.[2] An MRA/ARA may be issued when the President of

---

[1]The BCC is a group of informed futures professionals and non-members of the NFA that makes decisions about actions brought against NFA members.
[2]See NFA Manual, NFA Rule 3-2(c). Investigation.

the NFA, with the concurrence of the NFA's Board of Directors or Executive Committee, has reason to believe immediate action is necessary to protect the commodity futures markets, customers, or other NFA members or associates. Although not considered a formal disciplinary action, Part 3 of the NFA's Compliance Rules also authorizes the BCC to issue – or to authorize the Compliance Department to issue – a warning letter if, after completing an investigation, the NFA's Compliance Department concludes there is no reason to believe that an NFA requirement is being, has been, or is about to be violated, but that the circumstances that formed the basis for the investigation warrant the member's attention and due diligence.[3]

10.2 HOW COMPLAINTS ARE TRIGGERED

According to Hirst, in recent years, the majority of the NFA's BCC complaints and MRAs have resulted from targeted examinations of problematic firms and individuals, identified by the NFA's Risk Management System which was enhanced in 2009. The NFA's Risk Management System evaluates a firm's risk based on a number of weighted factors gathered from information in the NFA's databases. These factors include the employment history of firms' principals and associated persons ("APs"), disciplinary history, financial information, number of APs, and number of customers. The NFA's Risk Management System allows the NFA to focus its resources on the most high-risk member firms.

In addition, many of the NFA's recent MRA/ARAs were prompted by "red flags" that the NFA identified which, upon further investigation, revealed fraudulent conduct that warranted immediate action. For example, a commodity pool operator ("CPO") member filed a pool quarterly report for the quarter ending September 30, 2011 which reported significant losses of more than 70 percent in July and 99 percent in August 2011. Yet, despite these losses and no significant capital additions, the pool reported an ending net asset value of more than $8 million, which was over $1 million more than the pool's net asset value at the beginning of the quarter. Based on this

---

[3] See NFA Manual, NFA Rule 3-2(b). Investigation.

suspicious information in the pool quarterly report, the NFA commenced an emergency exam which uncovered a fraudulent scheme to misappropriate millions of dollars from investors and resulted in the issuance of an MRA by the NFA that shut down the CPO's operations. The NFA referred this case to federal law enforcement which led to criminal charges being filed against the principal of the CPO who was later convicted and sentenced to $12^1/_2$ years in federal prison.

The NFA's enforcement cases can also result from other sources, including complaints from customers or other NFA members, analysis of financial statements, routine examinations, and referrals from other Agencies.

10.3 INVESTIGATIVE PROCESS

If the NFA identifies serious or repetitive violations of NFA Rules, the violations are brought to the attention of the NFA Enforcement Department. If the determination is made that the matter is appropriate for prosecution, NFA Enforcement will begin an investigation. If sufficient evidence is found in the investigation, a recommendation will be made to the BCC.

Generally, if there is evidence of a violation, a report is issued to the BCC, recommending that the BCC issue a complaint against a member firm and/or individual members. The BCC acts in the role of grand jury, determining whether a complaint should be issued. As is the case with a grand jury, it is rare that the BCC refuses to follow a recommendation to issue a complaint. The report issued to the BCC must include: (a) the reason the investigation was begun; (b) a summary of the complaint, if the investigation was begun as the result of a complaint; (c) the relevant facts; and (d) the recommendation regarding whether the BCC should proceed with the matter.

The report is reviewed by the BCC and within 30 days of receiving the report, the BCC has the option of closing the matter, if it finds: (1) no reasonable basis that a violation has occurred, is occurring, or is about to occur; or (2) that prosecution is otherwise unwarranted (in which case the BCC may issue or cause to be issued a warning letter).[4] The BCC also has the option to serve a written and dated complaint to the offending party, if it finds reason to believe that an NFA requirement is being, has been, or is about to be violated and that the matter should be adjudicated. A complaint issued by the BCC must: (a) state each NFA requirement alleged to have been violated, and (b) state each act or omission that constitutes the alleged violation. The NFA then advises the offending party, known as the respondent, in writing that: (a) the respondent must file a written answer to the complaint with the NFA, within 30 calendar days of the date of the complaint; (b) failure to file an answer shall be deemed an admission of the facts and legal conclusions contained in the complaint; (c) failure to respond to any allegation shall be deemed an admission of that allegation; and (d) failure to file an answer shall be deemed a waiver of hearing.[5]

10.4 SETTLEMENT

The NFA's Rules provide for settlement of an NFA disciplinary proceeding.[6] In fact, according to Hirst, the vast majority of the BCC cases that the NFA closes each year are settled prior to a hearing.

Under the NFA's Rules, any proposed offer of settlement from a respondent is submitted to the BCC at any time up until a chairperson of the Hearing Panel is appointed. After that date, any proposed settlement offer is submitted to the Hearing Panel. The BCC or Hearing Panel may accept or reject the offer as it deems appropriate. The NFA is also allowed to express its views with respect to the proposed settlement.

If the BCC or Hearing Panel accepts a settlement offer, it will issue a written Decision specifying each NFA requirement it has reason to believe is being, has been, or is about to be violated; any penalty imposed; and whether the settling party has admitted or denied any violation. A Decision on a settlement by the BCC or

---

[4]See NFA Manual, NFA Rule 3-2(c). Investigation.
[5]See NFA Manual, NFA Rule 3-4. Notice of Charges.
[6]See NFA Manual, NFA Rule 3-11. Settlement.

Hearing Panel is promptly furnished to the President of the NFA and will become final and binding 15 days after the date of the Decision unless the President, with notice to all parties, refers the matter to the NFA's Appeals Committee for review. The Appeals Committee must approve or disapprove the settlement within 30 days after the date of such referral and its decision to approve or disapprove the settlement shall become final and binding 15 days after the date of that decision.[7]

10.5 THE HEARING PANEL AND HEARING COMMITTEE

If no settlement is reached, the respondent is afforded a hearing on the charges and possible sanctions. The hearing shall be before a designated Hearing Panel of the Hearing Committee ("Hearing Panel"). According to Hirst, the NFA's Hearing Committee consists of at least 15 individuals who are NFA members or connected with NFA members (e.g., an employee of an NFA member firm) or members of the public. The members of the Hearing Panel are proposed by the President of the NFA and approved by the NFA's Board of Directors. The individuals proposed and appointed must reflect the various categories of NFA members and members of the public and must meet certain qualifications under NFA Bylaw 708 (e.g., may not have been convicted of a felony within the prior 10 years or subject to an MRA or ARA which is currently in effect). At least one-third of the members of the Hearing Committee must not be NFA members or associates or employees of NFA members. Each member of the Hearing Committee shall serve for three years, or until the member's death, resignation, ineligibility, or removal. No member of the Hearing Panel may participate in the matter if the member, or any person with which the member is connected, has a financial, personal, or other direct interest in the matter under consideration or is disqualified under NFA Bylaw 708. A Hearing Panel will consist of no fewer than three members of the Hearing Committee.

---

[7]See NFA Manual, NFA Rule 3-11(b). Settlement.

10.6   CONDUCT OF THE HEARING

The respondent is entitled to a pre-hearing examination of all evidence in the NFA's possession or under its control that is to be relied upon by the NFA or that is relevant to the complaint.[8] In addition, the NFA has the "right to withhold any privileged material (including, but not limited to, the investigation report), pursuant to all common law and statutory privileges it has available to it," (e.g., attorney/client privilege, work product privilege).[9] The pre-hearing examination must be requested by the respondent in writing, and can be conducted either by the respondent examining all evidence at the offices of the NFA, or by the respondent requesting that all evidence be copied and sent to him with any transportation and copying costs borne by the respondent making the request.[10]

According to Hirst, NFA Rules also provide for the filing of pre-hearing motions.[11] In particular, within 30 days after the appointment of the chairperson of the Hearing Panel, he or she will schedule and hold a pre-hearing conference with the parties. During the conference, which is usually conducted by telephone, the chairperson of the Hearing Panel will schedule the hearing and set discovery and motion deadlines. The chairperson of the Hearing Panel is responsible for deciding all pre-hearing motions concerning discovery, motion deadlines, hearing location, continuances, and requests for telephonic or video testimony. In addition, any motion for a continuance must be supported by an affidavit that provides a detailed description of the circumstances that form the basis for the continuance request. All other motions are decided by the Hearing Panel.

According to Hirst, discovery and continuance motions are somewhat common in NFA disciplinary proceedings. However, while motions to dismiss or for summary judgment are permitted, the filing of such motions at the NFA is extremely rare.

At the hearing, the formal rules of evidence do not necessarily apply. The respondent has the right to appear personally, examine

---

[8] See NFA Manual, NFA Rule 3-8(a). Pre-Hearing Procedures.

[9] See NFA Manual, NFA Rule 3-8(a)(iii). Pre-Hearing Procedures.

[10] See NFA Manual, NFA Rule 3-8(a). Pre-Hearing Procedures.

[11] See NFA Manual, NFA Rule 3-8(c). Pre-Hearing Procedures.

any witnesses, call witnesses, and present relevant testimony and other evidence. Any party to the hearing may request that an NFA member, associate, or person connected with the matter be required to testify or produce documents at a hearing subject to the discretion of the Hearing Panel.[12]

According to Hirst, one feature that is unique to an NFA disciplinary case is that a respondent may request to testify, and have witnesses testify, telephonically at a hearing subject to the approval of the Hearing Panel. In addition, Hirst notes that because of the high settlement rate of NFA disciplinary cases, hearings at the NFA are relatively rare, averaging two or three a year. The most hearings in a year occurred in 2010 when there were nine hearings.

10.7 WRITTEN DECISION AFTER THE HEARING

After the hearing, the Hearing Panel makes a written decision, based upon the weight of the evidence, containing: (a) the charges or a summary of the charges; (b) the answer of the respondent; (c) a brief summary of the evidence produced at the hearing; (d) a statement of findings and conclusions as to each allegation, including a statement setting forth each act or practice the respondent was found to have committed or omitted, each NFA requirement that such act or practice violated, and whether the act or practice is deemed to constitute conduct inconsistent with just and equitable principles of trade; (e) a declaration of any penalty imposed and the penalty's effective date; and (f) a statement that the respondent may appeal an adverse decision to the Appeals Committee by filing a written notice of appeal with the NFA within 15 days after the date of the decision.[13]

10.8 APPEAL OF AN ADVERSE DECISION

The respondent may appeal any adverse decision of the Hearing Panel to the Appeals Committee by filing a written notice of appeal with the NFA within 15 days after the date of the decision. The

---

[12] See NFA Manual, NFA Rule 3-9(d). Hearing.
[13] See NFA Manual, NFA Rule 3-10. Decision.

notice must describe those aspects of the disciplinary action to which exception is taken, and must contain any request by the respondent to present written or oral argument. The Appeals Committee may also order a review of any decision of the Hearing Panel on its own motion or pursuant to a petition filed by the NFA. If the respondent files a notice of appeal, the effect of the decision is stayed until the Appeals Committee renders its decision.[14]

If the Appeals Committee authorizes written argument, briefs are filed by both parties. The Appeals Committee then issues a written decision, which must include: (a) the findings and conclusions of the Appeals Committee as to each charge and penalty reviewed, including the specific NFA requirement the respondent was found by the Hearing Panel to have violated, to be violating, or to be about to violate; and (b) a declaration of any penalty imposed by the Appeals Committee, the basis for its imposition, and its effective date.

The Appeals Committee Decision becomes final 30 days after the date of service on the parties, subject to review by the CFTC. In addition, the Appeals Committee may increase, decrease, or set aside the penalties that were imposed by the Hearing Panel, or may impose other and different penalties, as it sees fit, subject to the requirements and limitations set forth under NFA Rule 3-14(a). According to Hirst, after exhausting an appeal at the NFA, a respondent in an NFA disciplinary case may appeal an adverse Decision to the CFTC and ultimately to the federal courts – although this has happened very infrequently.

10.9 THE MRA PROCEDURE

According to Hirst, an MRA is a summary action where an NFA member (or associate) may be summarily suspended from membership or association with a member; may be required to restrict operations (e.g., restrictions on accepting new accounts); or may be otherwise directed to take remedial action (e.g., infuse additional capital).

---

[14]See NFA Manual, NFA Rule 3-13. Appeal; Review.

If an MRA is taken, the respondent is generally served with a notice before the action is taken. The notice includes: (a) the action taken or to be taken; (b) the reasons for the action; (c) the time and date when the action became effective and its duration; and (d) the statement that any person aggrieved by the action may petition for a stay of the effective date of the action pending a hearing. If it is not practicable to hold a hearing before the MRA is taken, the member or associate will be afforded an opportunity for a hearing before the Hearing Committee as promptly as possible.[15] There is no discovery in MRA proceedings.

After the hearing, the Hearing Panel issues a written decision affirming, modifying, or reversing the action taken, based upon the evidence contained in the record of the proceeding. The decision must contain: (a) a description of the action taken and the reasons for the action; (b) a brief summary of the evidence received at the hearing; (c) findings and conclusions; and (d) a determination as to whether the summary action that was taken should be affirmed, modified, or reversed and a declaration of any action to be taken against the respondent as the result of that determination. The respondent does not have the right to appeal an MRA action to the Appeals Committee.[16]

10.10 TYPES OF PENALTIES ASSESSED BY THE NFA

The types of penalties that may be assessed in the disciplinary process include: (a) expulsion, or suspension for a specified period, from NFA membership; (b) bar or suspension for a specified period from association with an NFA member; (c) censure or reprimand; (d) a monetary fine, not to exceed $250,000 per violation; (e) an Order to cease and desist; and (f) any other fitting penalty or remedial action.[17]

---

[15]See NFA Manual, NFA Rule 3-15. Member or Associate Responsibility Actions.
[16]See ibid.
[17]See NFA Manual, NFA Rule 3-14. Penalties.

The BCC, Hearing Committee, Appeals Committee, and BCC Hearing Panel conducting proceedings must include at least one member who is not an NFA member or associate or an employee of an NFA member.[18]

10.11 NUMBER AND TYPES OF DISCIPLINARY ACTIONS

According to Hirst, on average, the NFA issues approximately 40 disciplinary complaints and seven MRA/ARAs each year. Over the past 10 years (2005–2014), the NFA has issued over 400 complaints and 65 MRA/ARAs. The types of disciplinary actions brought by the NFA in 2014 included claims of fraud or misrepresentations such as:

- Committing fraud and exercising discretion over customers' accounts without written authority.
- Willfully providing misleading information to pool participants.
- Misrepresenting assets under management.
- Making misleading representations to the public.
- Engaging in deceptive, misleading, and high-pressure sales solicitations.

In 2014, the NFA also brought actions relating to failures to provide required information to the NFA or to cooperate with the NFA, such as claims alleging:

- Willful submitting of misleading information to the NFA.
- Failing to cooperate promptly and fully with the NFA during its examination.
- Providing false information to the NFA.
- Failing to complete the NFA's self-examination checklist.
- Omitting required information from a disclosure document.

---

[18] See NFA Manual, NFA Rule 3-17. Composition of Committees.

- Failing to report changes to application information.
- Failing to file telegraphic notice with the NFA in a timely manner notifying the NFA of the deficiencies.
- Failing to report trade data and other required information to the NFA in a timely fashion.
- Failing to file a disclosure document or annual financial statement for the fund with the NFA.

The NFA has also asserted claims for failures to implement required programs or develop mandated plans and policies, including:

- Failing to implement an adequate AML program by failing to have an annual independent audit performed of the firm's AML program or conduct AML training.
- Failing to establish adequate procedures regarding ethics training.
- Failing to develop a business continuity/disaster recovery plan.
- Failing to develop and maintain a privacy policy.

Claims were also asserted by the NFA in 2014 for matters related to promotional materials, such as:

- Failing to reference in promotional materials that past results are not necessarily indicative of future results.
- Using hypothetical trading results without identifying such results as hypothetical, or when actual results existed.
- Failing to provide an approved disclosure document to a customer.

Other actions have been brought for failures to comply with basic NFA requirements, such as:

- Doing business with a non-member of the NFA that was required to register with the CFTC.
- Failing to maintain adequate books and records.

- Permitting a commodity pool to make loans or advances to its commodity pool operator.
- Permitting an individual to act as an Associated Person ("AP") without sponsoring the individual as an AP of the firm.
- Failing to terminate APs.
- Failing to prepare net capital computations in a timely manner.
- Failing to maintain the required minimum adjusted net capital.
- Failing to comply with the equity withdrawal restriction.
- Failing to keep accurate financial records.
- Failing to comply with the equity withdrawal restriction.
- Failure to implement an adequate customer identification program for customers introduced to foreign brokers.
- Conducting futures business with a suspended associate.
- Failing to furnish participants in the fund with a financial statement.
- Failing to comply with CPO quarterly reporting requirements.
- Doing business with an unregistered entity or a suspended NFA associate.
- Attempting to conceal capital contributions from an unlisted principal.
- Failing to meet the firm's secured amount requirement.

In a majority of these proceedings, settlements were entered into between the NFA and the respondents. The settlements agreed to or findings made after a hearing included:

- Fines, ranging from $5,000 to $50,000.
- An Order to pay restitution of over $100,000 to customers.
- Permanent bar from NFA membership.
- Temporary withdrawal from NFA membership, with an agreement not to reapply for a specified period of time.
- An Order not to manage any discretionary accounts or act in a supervisory capacity for one year.
- An Order to tape record, for one year, all conversations with existing or potential customers, retain the tapes for one year, and make the tapes available to the NFA upon request.

10.12 TRENDS IN NFA ENFORCEMENT

According to Hirst, historically, the vast majority of the NFA's disciplinary cases involved fraudulent and misleading advertising and sales solicitations employed by boiler room operations, many of which were concentrated in south Florida. To a large extent these boiler room operations have been put out of business or have migrated from the futures industry into other areas. More recently, the NFA's disciplinary cases have focused on abusive trading recommendations, improper pricing practices involving forex trading platforms, prohibited loans from commodity pools to their pool operators, lax internal controls at member firms, and deficient anti-money laundering procedures and practices.

10.13 PREPARING A DEFENSE

As the NFA does not issue that many complaints in a given year, in my view, defendants in NFA Enforcement proceedings have a great deal of information that they can utilize to assist their defense. Conducting research on previous NFA actions, with the assistance of experienced counsel, can be very helpful in understanding the strategy and approach of the NFA examiners. Understanding the types of Enforcement cases traditionally brought by the NFA and incorporating this information into a firm's compliance program can also be useful in ensuring that firms never even get to the position of being a defendant in an NFA Enforcement proceeding.

CHAPTER 11

How to Participate in the Regulatory Comment Process

While companies and firms faced with the myriad of oftentimes overlapping regulations are generally in a defensive posture with respect to examinations or Enforcement actions, there are ways in which companies can act in a proactive manner to attempt to change the regulatory guidelines to assist their businesses or reduce their liabilities. This can sometimes be accomplished through commenting on the regulatory rulemaking process.

11.1 DODD-FRANK RULEMAKING

Pursuant to the Dodd-Frank Act, federal Agencies, including the SEC and CFTC, have been charged with promulgating hundreds of rules to bring the Dodd-Frank Act to life and determine the intention of the statute and how it will be implemented. These rules, many of which are hundreds of pages long, carry the force and effect of law and impose requirements that are just as binding as those directly imposed by the statute.

The rulemaking process is, for the most part, a transparent one, which allows interested individuals and firms to impact the process by providing comments to the regulatory Agency to address the issues that are contained in the rules. In addition, once a rule has been finalized, affected parties are able to sue the promulgating

Agency for acting arbitrarily, violating procedural requirements, or regulating beyond their statutory authority.

11.2 SEC RULEMAKING PROCESS

For the SEC, the rulemaking process involves the following several steps: concept release, rule proposal, and rule adoption. While the rulemaking process often begins with a rule proposal, sometimes an issue is so unique and/or complicated that the SEC seeks out public input on which, if any, regulatory approach is appropriate. In these instances, a concept release is issued describing the area of interest and the SEC's concerns and identifying different approaches to addressing the problem, followed by a series of questions that seek the views of the public on the issue. The public's feedback is then taken into consideration as the SEC decides which approach is appropriate.

In the second step, the SEC publishes a detailed formal rule proposal for public comment. Unlike a concept release, a rule proposal advances specific objectives and methods for achieving them. Typically the SEC provides between 30 and 60 days for review and comment. Just as with a concept release, the public comment is considered when the SEC determines how to formulate a final rule.

Finally, the SEC considers what it has learned from the public exposure of the proposed rule, and seeks to agree on the specifics of a final rule. If a final measure is then adopted by the SEC, it becomes part of the official rules that govern the securities industry.[1]

Jay Knight, a partner in the law firm of Bass, Berry & Sims, whose law practice includes counseling companies on regulatory reporting matters, and who previously held several positions in the SEC's Division of Corporation Finance, including as a member of the SEC Dodd-Frank Implementation Team, where he led a team of attorneys, economists, and accountants charged with implementing rulemaking projects under the Dodd-Frank Act, believes that comment letters on regulatory matters can be very effective. Knight states that, in the rulemakings he was involved in when he worked at

---

[1] See http://www.sec.gov/about/whatwedo.shtml#.VK6x09hOW70.

the SEC, there was a great deal of focus on the part of SEC officials on what the commenters said about the issues, and he felt that the comments he received were very helpful when trying to craft the final rule. Knight further states that he has often seen changes in the final rule based upon the comments made by the public, and notes that, particularly at the SEC, there will be extensive footnotes in the SEC's final rules citing to comment letters, and indicating that the revision made often reflects the view that a majority of the commenters expressed.

11.3   CANDIDATES FOR COMMENTS

Knight states that the concept releases and rule proposals are prime candidates for comments. When a concept release is issued, Knight explains that there is a desire for the Agency to learn more about a particular area. In this instance, the Agency believes that rulemaking is needed in this area but is trying to get feedback from the public on what the proposed rule should look like. This is a release where the Agency more than anything else is asking for public input on a particular topic and therefore is ripe for public comment. In addition, according to Knight, the rule proposal itself (also known as the notice of proposed rulemaking ("NPR") by some federal Agencies[2]) is the most common form that will elicit comments from the public.

11.4   ROLE OF TRADE ASSOCIATION IN COMMENT PROCESS

Some companies utilize trade associations to submit comments on their behalf about issues of common interest. Knight explains that some companies like the comfort in numbers that comes with a trade association where you can vocalize your viewpoint and not be singled out. In those situations, companies also receive the collective benefit of others in the industry. However, Knight counsels that if a company has a strong viewpoint on a particular issue, and they do

[2]Generally, banking regulators use the NPR term, while the SEC refers to a rule proposal as a "proposed rule" or "proposing release."

not consider it an issue that will negatively impact the reputation of the company, it could be helpful to the company to get out in front of the issue and individually submit a comment letter. In addition, as a trade association's comment may need to present a compromise position because it is representing the viewpoint of many companies in an industry, if a company is concerned about its position being watered down or compromised too much, Knight recommends that the company submit its own letter and talk to the Agency staff on its own. Knight does not believe that there is an actual risk for a company to put forward their own comments about an issue in normal circumstances, noting that he has read thousands of comment letters and has never seen any discussion that a company was targeted or harmed by what it stated in its comments.

Knight notes that issuing a comment letter, whether through a trade association or simply several interested parties writing together, can often carry more weight than an individual comment. However, it is very common for interested parties to submit their own letters and those can be very helpful to an Agency as well. Further, Knight explains that an Agency final rule can be swayed by individual comments as they can be very persuasive as well.

Members of trade associations often submit form letters to an Agency attempting to demonstrate that many different people advocate a certain position in a rulemaking. Knight states that these form letters can sometimes have an additional impact if they are also sent to Congressional officials in addition to the Agency involved in the rulemaking. Sending hundreds or even thousands of form letters to a Congressman or Senator's office can demonstrate that a large number of the representatives' constituents feel strongly about a particular subject. This can result in political pressure being placed on an Agency that can impact a rulemaking. According to Knight, it is not uncommon for the Chairman of the SEC to receive a letter from one or even several Senators or Congressmen regarding a particular rulemaking. Knight explains that many of the rulemakings are promulgated under the authority that the SEC received from Congress, as with the many regulations implementing the Dodd-Frank Act. Accordingly, members of Congress may attempt to influence the SEC with respect to this particular viewpoint on a rulemaking, and the element of politics can, depending upon the circumstances, have an impact on the SEC's final rule. Therefore, it may be advisable for the trade association to provide interested parties on Capitol Hill copies of comments submitted to a regulatory Agency.

A comment letter should always include the docket number of the regulatory proposal at the top of the document and may include an introduction which describes the company size, location, and business activities and explains the nexus between the company and the proposed regulation.

11.5 CONTENT OF THE COMMENT LETTER

Knight advises that if the comment letter is particularly long and covers many different issues within the rulemaking, it is helpful to have an executive summary. If the comment letter is relatively short, for example, fewer than five pages, a summary may not be needed. Knight explains, though, that a regulatory Agency like the SEC will read the entire comment letter no matter how long or short it is. In fact, there will likely be at least two individuals who will read every single comment letter that is submitted. Generally, Knight explains that there are typically one or two people that are the staff-level quarterback, i.e., those who take the lead on the particular rulemaking. The staff-level quarterback and his or her colleagues would then summarize all the comment letters that were submitted. If the letter is deemed particularly significant, the comment letter will also be read by senior-level Agency officials. If there is a meeting with a commenter, the commenter's letter will likely be read by all the participants in the meeting. On some rulemakings, the SEC would have as many as 15 staffers working on reviewing the comments and drafting the rule. The SEC also usually includes in-house economists and accountants on certain rules or other experts within the SEC.

Knight explains that in his view there is no minimum or maximum length for a comment letter. However, his advice in general is to be as succinct and clear as possible in a submission. He has seen instances where comment letters are written like legal briefs and where points are made over and over again, and counsels commenters to try to get to the point as quickly as possible, with the understanding that the Agency staffers will be tasked with reading hundreds, if not thousands, of comment submissions. Knight says that if a comment letter contains needless verbiage for the sake of writing a long letter, it is not beneficial to anyone. Knight also explains that commenters should keep in mind that the Agency staffers may not be as familiar with the commenter's business as the commenters are, and therefore, it is preferable for the comment letter to explain the issue in a simple manner with the assumption that the reader is not working in that business or industry. For example it can be helpful, in some cases, for a company to explain its internal structure in the comment letter. In addition, Knight recommends attaching an explanatory diagram or other illustration to the comment letter if it can be useful to explain a complex concept.

Knight explains that there is no requirement for a commenter to respond to every question in a concept or proposing release. If there are 100 questions in a concept release, and the commenter only has interest in two or three of them, the commenter should only answer those two or three. Knight also advises that if the concept release or rule proposal includes specific questions it may be helpful for the commenter to respond specifically to the questions presented in a question/answer format to make it easier for the Agency staffer to understand the comment being submitted. The commenter also should be clear about which positions the commenter agrees with and which are the ones with which they disagree.

In a similar vein, Knight advises that commenters focus on the issues with which they are most concerned and affected. If a rule-making has ten issues, and the commenter actually has a concern or comment on all ten of them, the commenter should, by all means, make a comment on all ten of them. However, if there are really only four in which a genuine interest exists, or that would have an impact on the commenter's business, only those issues should be raised.

It is also good advice, according to Knight, to incorporate some positive feedback in the commenter's submission when appropriate from the viewpoint of the commenter. While it is not required to "stand up and applaud" everything the commenter agrees with, when the Agency staff is weighing whether or not to keep a particular part of the rule in the final version, they are going to be weighing who agrees with it and who disagrees with it. Knight notes that if everyone who disagrees with a particular section of the rule says they disagree with it, but no one who comments affirmatively states they agree with the section of the rule because they think, "Oh, we agree with it, so we just do not need to say it," then this could result in the Agency staff not receiving a full and accurate picture of the public's views. Therefore, if a commenter agrees with a portion or section of the proposed rule, it would behoove him or her to indicate this fact clearly in the submission.

Providing possible alternative approaches to a concept discussed in the proposed rule can also be very helpful to the regulator according to Knight, who notes that there is no monopoly by the Agency officials writing the rules on the best way to achieve the outcome. Accordingly, the regulator will generally welcome feedback if the commenters provide a better way to achieve the goal of the rule-making than is presented in the proposed rule. From an Agency perspective, Knight explains that all options are on the table and if there is a feature that would make the rulemaking much simpler to implement from an industry perspective, this information should be brought to the Agency staff's attention. Knight states that every rulemaking he has been a part of has been improved, in some way, because of options and alternatives that were not initially mentioned in the release. In those instances, industry representatives came to the SEC and stated: "We think we know what you are trying to achieve. Here is another way to do it that we think achieves the principle behind the rule."

Knight notes that it is also helpful in a comment submission to attempt to refute the position of those who will be advocating the opposite side. Often, Knight notes that this is difficult to do because many commenters wait until the last day to submit their comments. However, if the other side's position is known, it should be addressed as one does not want to argue one's own position and disregard what the counterargument would be. When refuting another position, it is important to use measured language and avoid politically charged rhetoric. Agencies do not respond well to rants, and if the language is seen as demeaning another position or commenter, the comment will lose much of its persuasiveness.

11.6 APPROACHES TO AN EFFECTIVE COMMENT LETTER

In attempting to put forward a persuasive comment, one may take several different approaches. One can tie the comments to a particular economic impact, such as a loss of jobs, or in the alternative, one may make a more policy or theoretical argument. Knight believes that either of these approaches can be effective depending on the circumstances. He does note that over the past several years, rulemakings have been particularly focused on economic impacts. Accordingly, information about the economic impact of a rule can be very helpful, particularly if data can be included that supports the positions being taken. Knight notes that these arguments and the data can be particularly useful and persuasive for the economists who are often working on the rulemaking. Knight explains that in the past, the discussion about the economic impact in many rulemakings was relegated to the back of the document describing the Agency's response to comments. In recent years, the impact of the rule, in an economic sense, is being weaved into the policymaking discussions.

11.7 SIGNIFICANCE OF THE ECONOMIC IMPACT OF PROPOSED REGULATIONS

In the past several years, some of the reasons that financial Agencies have been much more attuned to the economic impact of proposed regulations, particularly regulations implementing the Dodd-Frank Act, relate to pressure from Congress and successful lawsuits brought challenging implemented rules. When I served as Inspector General of the SEC, I was asked by Congressional committees on more than one occasion to conduct an analysis of whether the SEC was appropriately incorporating economic impacts into its rules implementing the Dodd-Frank Act. My counterparts at the CFTC and other financial Agencies were also tasked with conducting this type of analysis.

In one of my office's reviews, I found that the extent of the SEC's quantitative discussion of cost-benefit analyses varied among rulemakings and that none of the rulemakings we had examined in a part of our review had attempted to quantify either benefits or costs other than information collection costs as required by the Paperwork Reduction Act.[3] We also found that some SEC Dodd-Frank Act rulemakings lacked clear, explicit explanations of the justification for regulatory action.[4] I also testified at several Congressional hearings about the extent to which Agencies were factoring the economic impact of Dodd-Frank implementing rules into their determinations.

In addition, business groups have had some success challenging SEC rules on the basis of lack of economic analysis. For example, in 2011, a federal appeals court invalidated an SEC proxy access rule permitting eligible shareholders to name director nominees in a company's proxy materials. The U.S. Chamber of Commerce and the Business Roundtable filed suit to challenge the rule, and a three-judge panel of the U.S. Court of Appeals for the District of Columbia found that the SEC inconsistently and opportunistically framed the costs and benefits of the rule, failed to adequately quantify certain costs or to explain why those costs could not be quantified, and arbitrarily acted in not evaluating the costs that could be imposed on companies from the use of the rule by certain parties.[5]

When including information on the economic or financial impact of a rule, it can be helpful to incorporate company-related financial information, such as the specific costs of implementing the rule. Knight advises in this scenario to include some sense of relative scale to demonstrate the specific burden on the company of implementation. As the Paperwork Reduction Act requirement in all rulemakings compels Agencies to address certain burdens of the rule

---

[3]The Paperwork Reduction Act (44 U.S.C. 3501-3520) requires Agencies to solicit and review public comments on the "collection of information" requirements of proposed rules and requires that Agencies evaluate the need for the collection of information and provide a specific, objectively supported estimate of the burdens of the information collection triggered by the rule.

[4]See full Office of Inspector General report at http://www.sec.gov/about/offices/oig/reports/audits/2012/rpt499_followupreviewofd-f_costbenefitanalyses_508.pdf.

[5]See the full D.C. Circuit Court decision at http://www.cadc.uscourts.gov/internet/opinions.nsf/89BE4D084BA5EBDA852578D5004FBBBE/$file/10-1305-1320103.pdf.

being proposed, providing specific numbers quantifying these burdens can be very important. Knight notes that from the regulator's perspective, there is a benefit to the rule, which is why the staff recommended it in the first place. The regulator also understands that there are obviously costs to every rulemaking. However, Knight explains that what this actually means in practice, in the form of an actual number or calculation, even if it is a range or estimate, can greatly assist the decisionmakers in understanding the true costs of the rule.

It is also helpful to be as specific as possible in describing the burdens caused by the regulation. One could include information that suggests that implementation of the regulation would result in the company expending additional resources on personnel time, equipment, training, recordkeeping, or simply result in the company changing its processes to comply with the regulation in a manner that does not advance the goals of the regulation. These additional burdens should be translated into specific costs, including the specific amount of salary or wages that employees would be paid to comply with the rule, together with specific additional costs of new equipment as well as personnel, training, recordkeeping, etc.

In addition to specific information regarding a company's costs, providing data across the industry would be ideal if such information is available. Knight notes, however, that it is often difficult to quantify the impact of a rule and sometimes studies may be subject to so many assumptions that they are no longer considered useful to the regulators.

11.8 REQUESTING MEETINGS WITH AGENCY OFFICIALS

In addition to submitting comments, Knight notes that interested parties may wish to ask to schedule meetings with Agency staffers working on the rulemaking to further express their positions. Knight notes that meetings are fairly common and typically are scheduled after the comment period ends. Knight advises that commenters call the Agency staffers identified in the proposed rule and ask if they are available for a short meeting of approximately 30 minutes to an hour. Knight explains that the meetings will be part of the public record and there will be a one-page memorandum prepared by the Agency staff describing what occurred at the meeting that will be posted to the SEC website that discusses the rulemaking. In addition, if one hands out slides or written materials to the staff and leaves them with the staff, those materials will also be posted to the SEC website with the memorandum.

If one does not wish to have the written materials publicly disclosed, one may, according to Knight, hand the materials to the staff for the purposes of the meeting but then take them back before leaving the meeting. It is also advisable to follow up with the staff after the meeting with a written submission, particularly if the positions expressed in the meeting are different from those described in the previously submitted comment letter. Agency staff ordinarily cannot rely upon oral comments alone and therefore, if there are substantive points to be made in addition to the positions taken in the comment letter, they must be provided in writing to be considered.

Meetings can also be requested with senior-level Agency officials, including Commissioners or Commission staff.

11.9 SUBMITTING COMMENTS AFTER THE DEADLINE

Knight notes that even if one missed the deadline for submitting comments to a proposed rule, one can still submit a comment letter, and the submission is still likely to be considered as long as it is received prior to the SEC action. The general policy of the SEC, for example, is to consider anything provided by the public up until the date the final rule is issued.

11.10 LEARNING ABOUT RULEMAKINGS

Knight says that companies can learn about regulatory rulemakings that may impact them from trade associations and law firms that monitor the regulators and inform their clients or potential clients in the industry about rulemakings. He also recommends that in-house counsel keep up-to-date on rulemakings and monitor releases for opportunities to provide comments.

11.11 ASSISTANCE FROM OUTSIDE COUNSEL

Knight also recommends in certain situations that companies retain outside counsel who are experienced in the regulatory process or the rule that is being promulgated to assist in preparing comment letters. Knight explains that outside counsel may be particularly useful in drafting specific regulatory language of the rule that may be consistent with the company's position. If the company is suggesting a new alternative to the regulator, providing explicit language for the regulator to use in the final rule can be very effective. Counsel can also assist in reviewing draft comment letters before they are submitted.

CHAPTER 12

How to Defend FCPA Claims

C ongress enacted the U.S. Foreign Corrupt Practices Act (the "FCPA") in 1977 in response to revelations of bribery of foreign officials by U.S. companies.[1] The FCPA which has as its purpose to promote transparency in international transactions, especially between businesses and government, has historically led to significant penalties for both companies and increasingly, *individual* corporate representatives.

Under the FCPA, firms who are operating in the U.S. face charges in the U.S. for any laws their subsidiaries violate in a foreign country. In addition, the FCPA makes the organization liable even for the actions committed by its third-party agents. The FCPA is one of the most emphasized enforcement areas for both the DOJ and SEC and can be very challenging for companies to defend.

12.1 FCPA PROVISIONS

The FCPA contains both anti-bribery and accounting provisions. The anti-bribery provisions prohibit corrupt payments to foreign officials, parties, or candidates to assist in obtaining or retaining business or securing any improper advantage. The accounting provisions require companies to make and keep accurate books and records and to devise and maintain an adequate system of internal

---

[1] 15 U.S.C. §§ 78dd-1, *et seq.*

accounting controls. The accounting provisions also prohibit individuals and businesses from knowingly falsifying books and records or knowingly circumventing or failing to implement a system of internal controls.

12.2 FCPA ENFORCEMENT AUTHORITY

The DOJ and the SEC share FCPA enforcement authority.[2] The DOJ has criminal FCPA enforcement authority over public companies and their officers, directors, employees, agents, or stockholders acting on their behalf. The DOJ also has both criminal and civil enforcement responsibility for the FCPA's anti-bribery provisions over U.S. citizens, U.S. businesses, and their officers, directors, employees, agents, or stockholders acting on their behalf as well as foreign persons and businesses that act in furtherance of an FCPA violation while in the United States. Within the DOJ, the Fraud Section of the Criminal Division has primary responsibility for FCPA matters.

The SEC is responsible for civil enforcement of the FCPA over public companies and their officers, directors, employees, agents, or stockholders acting on their behalf. The SEC's Division of Enforcement has responsibility for investigating and prosecuting FCPA violations. In 2010, the SEC's Enforcement Division created a specialized FCPA Unit, with attorneys in Washington, D.C. and in regional offices around the country, to focus specifically on FCPA enforcement.[3]

The DOJ's FCPA Unit regularly works with the Federal Bureau of Investigation ("FBI") to investigate potential FCPA violations. The FBI's International Corruption Unit has primary responsibility for international corruption and fraud investigations and coordinates the FBI's national FCPA enforcement program. The FBI also has a dedicated FCPA squad of FBI special agents that is responsible for investigating the FBI's FCPA investigations. In addition, the Department of Homeland Security and the Internal Revenue Service

---

[2] See http://www.justice.gov/criminal/fraud/fcpa/guidance/guide.pdf.
[3] See http://www.sec.gov/news/press/2010/2010-5.htm.

Criminal Investigation unit regularly investigate potential FCPA violations.[4]

12.3 VIOLATIONS OF THE FCPA

A violation of the FCPA anti-bribery prohibition consists of several elements:

- A payment, offer, authorization, or promise to pay money or anything of value to a foreign government official, or to any other person …
- Knowing that the payment or promise will be passed on to a foreign official …
- With a corrupt motive …
- In order to assist the company in obtaining or retaining business or in directing business to any person or to secure an improper advantage.[5]

The FCPA's anti-bribery provisions apply to three categories of persons: (1) issuers; (2) domestic concerns; and (3) other persons who act in furtherance of the corrupt payment while in the United States. "Issuers" refer to companies whose securities are registered in the United States or which are required to file periodic reports with the SEC.[6] "Domestic concerns" means any individual who is a citizen of the United States and any corporation or other entity which has its principal place of business in the United States, or which is organized under the laws of a state of the United States.[7] The FCPA also applies to individuals who commit bribery on U.S. territory regardless of whether the person is a resident or does business in the U.S. U.S. corporations and nationals can be held liable for bribes

---

[4]See A Resource Guide to the U.S. Foreign Corrupt Practices Act By the Criminal Division of the U.S. Department of Justice and the Enforcement Division of the U.S. Securities and Exchange Commission, November 14, 2012 at http://www.justice.gov/criminal/fraud/fcpa/guidance/guide.pdf.

[5]15 U.S.C. §§ 78dd-1(a), 78dd-2(a), 78dd-3(a).

[6]15 U.S.C. § 78dd-1(a).

[7]15 U.S.C. § 78dd-2(h)(1).

paid to foreign officials even if no actions or decisions take place within the United States.

The definitions of "payment" and "foreign official" are broad and cover virtually any benefit conferred on someone in a position to affect a person's business dealings with a foreign government. Nonmonetary benefits, including travel and entertainment, are considered payments. The FCPA contains no monetary threshold; even the smallest bribes are prohibited. In fact, a bribe need not actually be paid in order to violate the law. Rather, the FCPA prohibits the mere offer, authorization, or promise to make a corrupt payment.

12.4 PENALTIES FOR VIOLATING THE FCPA

The penalties for violating the FCPA anti-bribery provisions can be harsh. Individuals face up to five years' imprisonment for each violation of the anti-bribery provisions of the FCPA, or up to 20 years for certain violations.[8] Corporations and other business entities may be fined up to $2 million for each violation, individuals as much as $100,000.[9] The maximum fine may be increased to $25 million for corporations and $5 million for individuals in the case of certain violations.[10]

12.5 FCPA EXEMPTIONS

The FCPA contains several provisions that exempt certain conduct from its anti-bribery provisions. The FCPA does not prohibit "facilitating or expediting payment[s]" made to foreign officials for the purpose of causing them to perform "routine governmental actions."[11] The distinction between a "facilitating payment" and a bribe is often difficult to determine. Payments to foreign officials for "routine governmental action," such as processing papers or issuing permits, in order to expedite performance of duties which they are already bound

---

[8] 15 U.S.C. § 78dd-1, §78 *et seq.*
[9] 15 U.S.C. § 78dd-1 *et seq.*
[10] 15 U.S.C. § 78ff(a).
[11] 15 U.S.C. §§ 78dd-1(b), 78dd-2(b), 78dd-3(b).

to perform and where the payments are not intended to influence the outcome of the official's action, but only its timing, are generally considered lawful facilitating payments.

The FCPA also does not prohibit payments that are lawful under the written laws and regulations of the foreign official's country.[12] The FCPA further provides that it is not a violation of the statute if the person charged can prove that the payment in question constituted "a reasonable and bona fide expenditure, such as travel and lodging expenses," in certain situations.[13]

12.6 DOJ/SEC GUIDANCE

In November 2012, the DOJ and the SEC released guidance on the criminal and civil enforcement provisions of the FCPA.[14] The Guide contains 10 chapters, which address the FCPA anti-bribery and accounting provisions, other related U.S. laws; the guiding principles of enforcement; penalties, sanctions, and remedies; resolutions; and whistleblowers. In addition, the Guide contains hypotheticals, examples of actual enforcement cases, and lists of factors and red flags to consider in addressing a number of FCPA issues.

The Guide emphasizes the importance that the DOJ and the SEC place on a strong corporate compliance program. The Guide enumerates 10 "Hallmarks of Effective Compliance Programs" as follows:

- A commitment from senior management and a clearly articulated policy against corruption.
- A code of conduct and compliance policies and procedures.
- Oversight of the compliance program by individuals who have appropriate authority within the organization and adequate resources to ensure implementation of the program.

---

[12] 15 U.S.C. §§ 78dd-1(c)(1), 78dd-2(c)(1), 78dd-3(c)(1).

[13] 15 U.S.C. §§ 78dd-1(c)(2), 78dd-2(c)(2), 78dd-3(c)(2).

[14] See A Resource Guide to the U.S. Foreign Corrupt Practices Act by the Criminal Division of the U.S. Department of Justice and the Enforcement Division of the U.S. Securities and Exchange Commission, November 14, 2012 at http://www.justice.gov/criminal/fraud/fcpa/guidance/guide.pdf.

- Risk assessment.
- Training in the FCPA policies and procedures throughout the organization.
- Disciplinary procedures and incentives.
- Third-party due diligence.
- Mechanisms for confidential reporting of misconduct and internal investigations of allegations brought to a company's attention.
- Continuous improvement through periodic testing and review.
- Pre-acquisition due diligence and post-acquisition integration for mergers and acquisitions.

Some elucidation is also provided by the Guide about the type of payments that are considered improper under the FCPA. Examples of improper payments given in the Guide include a $12,000 birthday trip for a government official that included visits to wineries and dinners; $10,000 worth of dinner, drinks, and entertainment for a government official; a trip to Italy for eight government officials, including $1,000 of pocket money for each official; and a trip to Paris for a government official and his wife that consisted primarily of touring activities with a chauffeur-driven vehicle. Although the FCPA does not have a *de minimis* monetary threshold, the Guide explains that items of nominal value (such as cab fares or promotional items) are unlikely to trigger liability without an intent to influence a foreign official.

The Guide also discusses the exception for "facilitating or expediting payments" made in furtherance of routine governmental action in the FCPA. It provides a few examples of what constitutes "routine governmental action" which are the circumstances in which the facilitating payments exception applies. The examples given are processing visas, providing police protection or mail services, and supplying utilities like phone services, power, and water. The Guide specifically provides that routine government action does not include a decision to award new business or to continue business with a particular party.

The Guide also explains that whether a payment falls within the "facilitating or expediting payments" exception is not necessarily dependent on the size of the payment, although the Guide notes that the size can be telling, as a large payment is more suggestive of corrupt intent to influence a non-routine governmental action. It emphasizes that the facilitating payments exception focuses on the purpose of the payment rather than its value. The Guide also notes that labeling a bribe as a "facilitating payment" in a company's books and records does not necessarily make it legal. It further warns that although facilitating payments are not illegal under the FCPA, they may still violate local law in the countries where the company is operating.

The Guide discusses that there are no guarantees that adopting an effective FCPA program will protect an organization from enforcement action. However, the Guide describes the government's commitment to providing favorable treatment to organizations that self-report, cooperate, and remediate when FCPA issues arise. It states that it will credit voluntary and timely disclosure of violations. The Guide provides specific examples of enforcement action that were not taken against companies who voluntarily disclosed violations, disciplined the responsible employees, and conducted a review of their compliance procedures.

12.7 THE U.K. BRIBERY ACT

In 2010, the United Kingdom enacted its own version of the FCPA, known as the U.K. Bribery Act. The U.K. Bribery Act prohibits bribery in both government and private commercial transactions. Under the U.K. Bribery Act, bribery is defined to occur when a person offers, promises, or gives a financial or other advantage to another person to induce the other person to perform, or reward the other person for performing, his or her job function improperly.[15] The prohibitions under the U.K. Bribery Act extend to individuals who agree to or receive a bribe as well as to individuals who offer or pay a bribe.[16]

---

[15] Section 1, U.K. Bribery Act 2010.
[16] Sections 1 and 2, U.K. Bribery Act 2010.

In addition, a commercial organization violates the U.K. Bribery Act if an individual bribes another individual with the intention of obtaining or retaining either business or a business advantage for that organization.[17] The U.K. courts have jurisdiction over bribery outside the United Kingdom where the person committing the violation is a British national or is ordinarily a resident of the U.K., an entity incorporated in the U.K., or a Scottish partnership.[18] In addition, any company that does business in the United Kingdom will be subject to the prohibitions against receiving a bribe with respect to conduct that occurs outside the United Kingdom, even where that conduct is unrelated to the U.K. aspect of its business. The U.K. Bribery Act also holds companies responsible for the improper actions of their employees and the third parties that act as intermediaries in their business transactions.[19] Unlike the FCPA, there is no exemption for facilitation payments. For individuals, the maximum penalty under the U.K. Bribery Act is 10 years' imprisonment and an unlimited fine.[20] For commercial organizations the penalty is an unlimited fine.[21]

12.8 DEVISING EFFECTIVE COMPLIANCE PROGRAMS

Devising an effective compliance policy is the best defense against FCPA and U.K. Bribery Act liability. Compliance programs must be tailored to fit the specifics of the company. Organizations should have an established set of compliance standards and procedures against violations of the FCPA, including its anti-bribery and accounting provisions, and the policy should be memorialized in a written compliance code.

Thomas Fox, an author of eight books on the FCPA and compliance, stresses the importance of having a robust compliance policy in place to deter FCPA problems or issues. Fox has practiced law in

---

[17] Section 7, U.K. Bribery Act 2010.
[18] Section 12, U.K. Bribery Act 2010.
[19] Section 7, U.K. Bribery Act 2010.
[20] Section 11, U.K. Bribery Act 2010.
[21] Ibid.

Houston for 30 years and assists companies with FCPA compliance programs. He previously served as the General Counsel at Drilling Controls, Inc., a worldwide oilfield manufacturing and service company and as Division Counsel with Halliburton Energy Services, Inc. Fox attended undergraduate school at the University of Texas, graduate school at Michigan State University, and law school at the University of Michigan. Fox writes and speaks nationally and internationally on FCPA compliance and other related issues. Fox notes that historically, the government has brought FCPA enforcement actions against companies who did not have a compliance program in place or they had one and ignored it.

12.9   TRAINING ON COMPLIANCE STANDARDS

There also needs to be training of employees, contractors, and subcontractors in the compliance standards and policies. The policies should be translated into the language of the employees who are supposed to be complying with them. Fox explains that the biggest mistake companies make with regard to training is not delivering the correct kind of training for the correct risk. He also emphasizes providing training to third parties, and putting mechanisms in place to assess if all employees and third parties have adequately received the training. Fox recommends that for the higher risk employees, training should be conducted in person because that is believed to be most effective as it emphasizes the importance of FCPA compliance and allows one to meet those employees face to face. For employees lower down the risk chain, Fox indicates that risk-based web training may be adequate.

12.10   ACHIEVING A CULTURE OF COMPLIANCE

Fox also emphasizes that in an FCPA action, the government will scrutinize a company's overall culture of compliance. The government will investigate the message being communicated from senior management to the rest of the employees. The government will look at whether the CCO really has authority and the resources to ensure compliance. One suggestion Fox makes is to have the CCO report directly to the CEO, the Board of Directors, and the Audit Committee, rather than having the CCO report to the General Counsel. This reporting technique will help in demonstrating independence and authority on the part of the CCO.

It is also essential to have an efficient and effective monitoring program because this is where government regulators tend to focus their investigations. Depending on the size of the company and the scope of its interactions with foreign government officials, monitoring should be led by a compliance officer or team. The government's position is that companies will be held liable for the conduct of their third parties, such as agents, consultants, and distributors. Moreover, it is often the case that third parties are used to conceal the payment of bribes to foreign officials in international business transactions.

12.11 RISK-BASED DUE DILIGENCE AND MONITORING

Risk-based due diligence and monitoring are particularly important with third parties. Companies should ensure they understand a third party's qualifications and associations, including its business reputation and relationships with foreign officials. Companies should also understand the business rationale for including a third party in a transaction. Ongoing monitoring of third-party relationships is critical to avoiding FCPA exposure.

In the monitoring efforts, one should pay particular attention to offices in countries where the risk of bribery is considered to be the highest, as well as the places where the company does the highest volume of business. According to Fox, the government wants a company's compliance program to do three things: (1) prevent violations; (2) detect violations; and (3) if a violation occurs, take action to remediate or fix the violation.

Fox recommends that companies' monitoring efforts include both forensic auditing and ongoing monitoring. According to Fox, monitoring is a shallower dive into large amounts of information and data. Forensic accounting and auditing, on the other hand, is a deeper dive into the information with a much narrower focus.

Fox stresses that the three most important things about FCPA compliance are: (1) document; (2) document; and (3) document, noting that if one does not document something, in the regulators' eyes, it never happened. One can have a paper compliance program but if the steps taken to implement the program are not documented, the government is going to assume you violated that program. The key, according to Fox, is to document that the policy and procedures were followed.

12.12 CONDUCTING FCPA COMPLIANCE ASSESSMENTS

Affirmative FCPA compliance assessments should also be conducted in order to make sure there are internal controls in place to catch and correct potential violations. Fox recommends that a gap analysis be performed to map out each step in the FCPA compliance program, to determine if there is sufficient review and oversight.[22] The purpose, according to Fox, is to determine whether there is sufficient discipline within the company to ensure that the required forms have been filled out completely and correctly and then submitted to the appropriate offices or individuals for review.

Fox indicates that the gap analysis or review should not be just a "check the box" review, but a thorough analysis of the information contained in the forms that are scrutinized. For example, if one is reviewing a company expense reimbursement form for an entertainment activity, Fox states that one needs to see written confirmation of the business purpose for the activity and an indication of whether or not the person taken out was a government official. Also, in that example, one would want to make sure that the spending limits for activities with government have not been exceeded both on a one-time basis and aggregated over a year. Fox notes that the key elements to look for in the gap analysis or review are whether there is sufficient financial control of the expense reimbursement form, and

---

[22] A gap analysis is part of a risk assessment that attempts to delineate the gaps between the areas where the company is complying fully with all rules and regulations and engaging in best practices, and where there are lapses or deficiencies.

whether the internal controls in place for the reimbursement form are tied into the company's compliance program so that if there is an FCPA violation, it is flagged by the compliance officials and dealt with appropriately.

12.13 IMPORTANCE OF RISK ASSESSMENT

A company's compliance program must be informed by its risk assessment and the program should be built around a company's individual and specific risks. Accordingly, in order to create an effective compliance program, one must identify and understand the risk factors systemic to the industry and unique to the company. These risk factors may relate to the geographic locations where the company is doing business, whether the company's potential customers are government Agencies or state-owned enterprises, and the types of individuals the company may utilize to obtain business overseas.

Fox notes that risk can be assessed by the following three measures: (1) where a company is doing business; (2) how the company is doing business; and (3) whom the company is doing business with. For (1), a good approach according to Fox is to look at the Transparency International Corruption Perceptions Index which delineates the countries with the highest corruption levels. For (2), Fox notes that 90 to 95 percent of all FCPA enforcement action involves third parties in some shape or form and thus, it is important to scrutinize whether your company works through agents, representatives, distributors, or other third parties that are not employees of your company, as they would represent a higher risk. For (3), Fox recommends analyzing the number and type of government interactions that a company has. For example, the energy industry is often an industry that is targeted by the government for FCPA violations. This occurrence is, according to Fox, because in the energy industry, companies are often interacting and doing business with governments. If the company wishes to extract minerals, for example, Fox notes that the company will likely enter into a contract with the government. If a company wants to go out and physically draw out or change a property, it is going to need a separate permit. If a company wants to get its equipment into the country, it is going to need to work through customs. Other industries that have a great deal of governmental interaction are the telecommunications and healthcare industries.

But Fox does not advise companies to avoid doing business in certain countries. He notes that the higher the risk level means the more that the risk must be managed. Even though there are countries that are generally rated as very high risk, such as Sudan or Somalia, one can conduct business with them by managing the increased risk. In addition, Fox gives the example of Angola, which is not rated as one of the higher risk countries, but because of a very limited educated class of workers, it is common in Angola for employees to go back and forth between working for the private sector and the government on a frequent basis, which presents an increased risk. However, Fox notes that even this type of risk can be managed if it is identified appropriately in advance.[23]

12.14 MANAGEMENT OF THIRD PARTIES

Fox also explains that the greatest risk for a company exists with regard to third parties.

Fox prescribes the following steps in the management of third parties.

- Having a business unit justification for doing business with the third party that explains why the company decided to do business with party A as opposed to party B.
- Requiring the third party to fill out a questionnaire consisting of information such as the identification of the ultimate beneficial owners of the company, the company structure, whether the company has ever been accused or found guilty of bribery or corruption, whether the company is generally aware of the FCPA, and whether the company has a code of conduct, or a compliance program. At that point, one should obtain references

---

[23]Of course, companies must also conduct a cost–benefit analysis to determine if the costs needed to be incurred in managing certain risks are worth the benefits of working in those countries or areas.

and from that information one can determine what level of due diligence to perform in step 3.

- Due diligence, which itself has three parts:
  - An online search of databases which identify bad actors such as politically exposed persons, terrorists, money launderers, and drug dealers;
  - An in-country database search and follow-up. Particularly in the international arena, this must be conducted in-country and in the local language;
  - Boots on the ground, which would involve sending individuals to the country to physically check records, e.g., in a courthouse, and to look at physical facilities themselves. This may also involve interviewing the principals of the proposed third-party agent to get a sense of their understanding of whether they understand the FCPA and what their obligations would be when working with a U.S. company. The information would be collected and analyzed for any red flags. If the red flags can be addressed credibly, one can move to the next step.
- After this due diligence has been evaluated and any red flags cleared you are ready to move to the contracting stage. The contract, which would include the commercial terms with the third party together with the compliance terms and conditions, must be carefully drafted. These compliance terms and conditions would include the following: (1) if there is an FCPA violation, the fact that this would constitute a material breach of contract and the contract would be terminated immediately; (2) an agreement to cooperate in any FCPA investigation; and (3) an agreement by the third party to allow the company to audit it from the compliance perspective. If the provisions of the contract are agreed to, one may move to the final step.
- Managing the relationship after the contract has been signed. According to Fox, this is the most important step because it may be incumbent on the company to educate the third party about the FCPA and what their obligations are. One needs to ensure that the third party documents its activities, that they have proper protocols in place, and that they certify on an annual basis that they have not engaged in any FCPA violations. In addition, one

must ensure that employees of the third party attend annual FCPA training, preferably in-person training conducted by a business unit representative on an annual visit to the country to emphasize the importance of the FCPA. Finally, it would be prudent to periodically audit the third party's books and records, including reviewing invoices that are submitted to make sure that there is nothing in the invoice that would indicate that they have paid a bribe on the company's behalf.

12.15 CONDUCTING DUE DILIGENCE ON ACQUISITION TARGETS

Another critical part of an FCPA compliance program is performing adequate due diligence on acquisition targets. In an acquisition or merger, the acquiring company will often inherit the liabilities of the target company. Accordingly, thorough due diligence for compliance with the FCPA must be a mandatory part of every transaction involving a foreign entity. In-house counsel must scrutinize the target company's interactions with public officials, including any actions taken by any third party on behalf of the target company. Such due diligence should include in-person interviews. FCPA due diligence must be conducted not only in acquisitions and joint ventures but also in any commercial transactions that a U.S. company conducts with a foreign entity or individual.

According to Fox, the most important thing for the acquiring company to do is to attempt a risk assessment on the target company. The DOJ made clear in Opinion Release 14-02, which came out in November 2014, that a company can avoid "purchasing a FCPA violation" by thoroughly vetting any target company.[24] This may be difficult as the acquiring company may be constrained and limited by the amount of data and information, and by the number of individuals made available for an interview from the target company. In a best case scenario, according to Fox, one should speak to the CEO, the CFO, the General Counsel, and the CCO, if the target company

---

[24]See full text of Opinion Release 14-02 at http://www.justice.gov/criminal/fraud/fcpa/opinion/2014/14-02.pdf.

has someone in that position. Fox also recommends reviewing the target's compliance program and their policies and procedures. In addition, if there is sufficient time, Fox suggests looking at the third parties that the target company does business with to see if they have been properly vetted. Finally, Fox recommends interviewing the employee sales people and the high-risk sales people.

Fox notes that the biggest problem with conducting due diligence in the pre-acquisition phase is that one never has enough time and generally not enough money to conduct a thorough and comprehensive review. Accordingly, it is helpful to do the things that will enable the acquiring company to get a sense of the target's general philosophy about business ethics and complying with the FCPA. However, with Opinion Release 14-02, the DOJ made clear the need for such pre-acquisition due diligence and not simply trying to clean things up post-acquisition.

12.16 THE TRIGGERS FOR AN FCPA ENFORCEMENT ACTION

In order to protect yourself from FCPA exposure, it is helpful to attempt to understand how the government obtains information that leads to FCPA Enforcement actions. According to Fox, the government investigates companies based upon the following three categories of information:

- The company self-reports or self-discloses an FCPA violation.
- A whistleblower comes forward and contacts the government with a potential violation of the FCPA. Fox notes that the whistleblower may be an employee of the company or a competitor.
- The "other" category, which may include governmental investigations in non-FCPA areas as well information, which foreign governments may provide to the U.S. government about bribery or corruption in their country. Fox says it could also include information that the U.S. government obtains through its spying efforts using satellites.

12.17 SELF-DISCLOSING VIOLATIONS

Even though companies may not have much control over whistle-blowers – particularly ones from competitors – or information the government learns either on its own or from foreign governments, companies can decide whether and in what circumstances it should self-disclose a violation. Although the government continually states that self-disclosure will lead to reduced penalties for cooperation, many are skeptical of whether companies actually benefit from self-disclosing FCPA violations. Fox states that he has heard conflicting messages from the U.S. government on the issue of self-disclosure. He notes that if you ever hear an official from the DOJ or SEC speaking, they will always tell you to self-disclose and they will highlight a couple of specific cases in which companies disclosed violations and were not criminally prosecuted. However, Fox points out that there have been cases where companies have not self-disclosed, but still received reduced penalties. Therefore, Fox believes that self-disclosing a violation may not be the only way a company can achieve credibility with the government and a lower penalty as a result since there have been cases where even if the violation was not self-reported by the company, it achieved a lower penalty by putting into place a strong remediation plan once the government notified them of their investigation. With respect to self-disclosure, Fox suggests that a company consider the following questions:

- How sure are they of the facts?
- Has the company thoroughly investigated what occurred?
- Has the company begun remediation efforts?

Fox notes that if a company self-discloses too early, the government may ask the company why it has not already started remediation. In that scenario, Fox points out that the government may actually end up directing the company's remediation efforts. In addition, according to Fox, a company might consider whether, if they have already remediated the problem, it makes sense, from a cost–benefit analysis, to disclose to the government and incur the cost of dealing with the government's investigation. Fox does warn that in today's world, one never really knows how the U.S. government gets information and if a company does not self-disclose, it runs the risk that the government is already aware of the issue and the company loses some credibility by failing to inform the government about the problem.

12.18 REDUCING EXPOSURE

Reducing or avoiding FCPA exposure can be very difficult because companies have less ability to control events overseas than they do in their offices in the U.S. Creating a robust compliance program with monitoring elements and ongoing training is an important start. It is important that if the government begins an investigation of the company, it sees a company committed on all levels to FCPA compliance. Documentation is critical to showing the government that the company takes the necessary actions to ensure that it is complying with all applicable laws.

If the company becomes aware of a potential violation of the FCPA, unless it is required by law to disclose it, it may want to give serious consideration to whether it should self-report to the government and the timing of any such reporting. In that scenario, it should act quickly to ensure that its policies and procedures are updated and that any potential remediation efforts have begun.

CHAPTER 13

How to Conduct Internal Investigations

The importance of conducting effective internal investigations as part of a company's overall compliance program cannot be overstated. Very often, company liability derives from an allegation initially raised internally which either is disclosed to a regulator or referenced in a lawsuit. These allegations can lead to Enforcement proceedings by any number of regulatory Agencies and even criminal exposure, particularly in the FCPA context.

13.1 LIMITING EXPOSURE THROUGH EFFECTIVE INTERNAL INVESTIGATIONS

Companies can effectively limit their legal exposure whether in the context of a potential FCPA claim or as a result of a whistleblower or other complaint by conducting a thorough and comprehensive internal investigation. A thorough, effective, and credible internal investigation is important not only so that the company understands fully what it is facing in terms of liability, but also to demonstrate to the regulatory authorities that it takes the complaints it receives seriously, and that it wishes to learn about potential problems within the company.

As discussed in Chapter 3, whistleblower complaints must be managed very carefully and it is critical that the whistleblower feel as if his or her complaints are being addressed and that follow-up is occurring on the specific allegations brought forward. In fact, whether the complaint is brought by a whistleblower or information is brought to the attention of the company through some other mechanism that needs follow-up investigatory work, companies must act quickly to investigate the allegations brought forward, and conduct the investigation in a credible and thorough manner.

13.2 LESSONS LEARNED FROM HIGH-PROFILE INVESTIGATIONS

In my tenures as Inspector General of both the Peace Corps and the SEC, I conducted many investigations, some of which were very high-profile, and I learned a great deal from these experiences. At the Peace Corps, my office conducted investigations of allegations of fraud on the part of Peace Corps Volunteers and embezzlement of public funds which were supposed to be used to assist indigent people all over the world. We also investigated allegations of rapes, assaults, and even murders of Peace Corps Volunteers serving in third-world countries.

At the SEC, I conducted the investigation of why the SEC failed to uncover Bernie Madoff's $50 billion Ponzi scheme, which involved interviewing approximately 140 witnesses (including Bernard Madoff himself) and the review of approximately 3.7 million e-mails over an eight-month period under incredible pressure from Congress and anticipation from the investing public. I followed that up with another investigation of a large Ponzi scheme, this time a $7 billion one perpetrated by Allen Stanford. I also conducted an audit/investigation of why Bear Stearns collapsed and other investigations relating to the financial crisis. In addition, I conducted many more mundane investigations at the SEC relating to employees failing to come to work, leaking confidential information to the media, and looking at pornographic images on their government computers during work hours.

In each investigation, I used a different approach or tactic to obtain the information needed. At the Peace Corps, particularly when I interviewed Peace Corps Volunteers, I often used a very informal approach. These Volunteers were mostly young, and had never been interviewed before by an investigator. I would interview them one-on-one either in my office or in a large, imposing conference room and stress to them the importance of telling the truth. I would ask them very direct questions, present them with the allegations or evidence that had been collected, and somewhat forcefully, but respectfully, attempt to obtain an admission or confession. At the conclusion of the interview, I would write up a statement for them, and get their signature on the statement before they left my offices. If the Volunteer had actually been guilty of the wrongdoing alleged, they would very often admit their culpability during the interview session and then I would factor their admission into the punishment recommended. If they were not responsible, but had information on others who were involved in misconduct, the approach I used would often elicit the damaging information about the other individual or individuals involved.

At the SEC, on nearly every occasion, I used a very different approach. Most of the witnesses I examined in my investigations at the SEC were either lawyers or accountants who were familiar with legal proceedings. Accordingly, I used a much more formal approach to conducting interviews. I arranged for a court reporter to transcribe the proceedings, and put the witnesses under oath. During the course of the interview, I often stressed the legal implications of providing false information to a federal investigator. I also used much more subtle approaches in my questioning, often relying upon documentary evidence that I would show the witnesses to elicit information that I was seeking. This approach was often very effective in obtaining truthful answers to questions and using the transcripts of early interviews to obtain information in later ones.

13.3 COMMENCING THE INTERNAL INVESTIGATION

The first issue that companies face when initiating an internal investigation is to determine who should undertake the investigation. If the issues seem relatively minor in nature, it makes sense for an in-house compliance unit or the General Counsel's office to conduct the investigation. The in-house personnel are already familiar with the company's policies, procedures, and systems and are in a good position to undertake a prompt investigation. However, these individuals must be trained in how to conduct investigations, including learning about the rights of employees who are being interviewed, and also understand appropriate and effective interview techniques.

Some believe that a lawyer who has a litigation background and has taken depositions and argued in court will have sufficient experience from his or her legal background to undertake an independent investigation. However, taking a deposition or cross-examining a witness in court is very different than conducting an interview in an investigation. The investigator must be completely impartial and non-biased and is simply seeking to learn information from witnesses, while in the deposition or trial context, the litigator is trying to obtain information that supports his or her client's positions. These are different skill-sets, and if an investigatory interview feels to the interviewee too much like a deposition, the interviewer's credibility may be impacted and the investigation may be tainted.

13.4 RETAINING AN OUTSIDE INVESTIGATOR

If the issues raised by a complaint could potentially amount to serious violations of law or could be viewed as firm-threatening in any way, it is better practice to hire an outside investigator to conduct the internal investigation. In this scenario, it is critical that the results of the investigation be viewed as credible. Having the investigation conducted by an individual or firm outside of the company provides a significant amount of credibility. This is the case as long as the outside individual or firm has no prior ties to the company. Retaining the company's long-time counsel to conduct the independent internal investigation erodes the credibility of the process. Companies should be very careful to choose an investigator who has not previously represented the company, and who does not have a reason to curry favor with the company.

One does not necessarily have to retain an attorney to conduct an internal investigation. Some non-attorney investigators have significant experience conducting investigations and have the particular skill-set of being able to elicit information from witnesses. If a non-attorney investigator is chosen, he or she should work under the direction of the legal counsel, however, to preserve the attorney-client privilege.

13.5 INITIAL STEPS OF INVESTIGATION PROCESS

Once the investigation is initiated, before taking any first steps, it is useful for the investigator to look at the "big picture" of the investigation and consider what information or evidence is needed to unravel the allegations and learn exactly what has occurred. One should consider all possible sources of information and try to think about what would be the most effective way to obtain the evidence needed.

In the Madoff investigation at the SEC, I immediately thought who would be better to provide me information concerning how the SEC was fooled by Bernie Madoff than Bernie Madoff himself? When I initially inquired about speaking with Madoff, I was told that I was wasting my time as he would never speak to me. I persevered and eventually interviewed him for approximately four hours in the Metropolitan Correctional Center in Manhattan, obtaining a great deal of information that was useful in my investigation and also establishing a higher level of credibility associated with my findings.

13.6 METHODS OF OBTAINING INFORMATION

The two primary ways of obtaining information in an investigation are through reviewing documents and conducting interviews of witnesses. In many ways, I have found that documentary evidence, particularly e-mails, can actually be more compelling evidence than personal interviews. In the many interviews I have conducted, especially when I was interviewing the subject of the investigation, I have found that witnesses often remember events the way they would like them to have occurred, rather than the way they actually happened.[1] In these instances, I firmly believe that the witnesses do not think they are

---

[1] For example, I have seen circumstances where witnesses recalled conferring with lawyers or ethics counsel before taking a certain action, when it was clear that they had not done so.

lying, as they have trained themselves to "truthfully" remember the events in such a way as to demonstrate that their actions were appropriate. On the other hand, documents such as e-mails are contemporaneous records of what occurred, and while, at times, documents need context to be completely understood, they present very valuable evidence, particularly of events that occurred years ago. When interviewing difficult witnesses, I often show them their own e-mails during the interview and ask them to explain the context surrounding the e-mails, as a way to elicit as much information as possible.

In one of my high-profile investigations, before I even asked my first question in an interview of the individual accused of wrongdoing in the investigation, he gave a very long speech challenging my right to question him and confidently assuring me that the interview was a complete waste of time on my part. I then began the interview by showing him a series of his own e-mails demonstrating ethical lapses on his part on several different occasions which changed his demeanor from one of haughtiness to a much more subdued and submissive tone. For the remainder of the interview, he was much less combative and I obtained useful information, including several admissions.

13.7 COLLECTING DOCUMENTS

The first substantive task in an investigation should be to identify and collect all available documents relevant to the allegations made. Initially, one should consider sending out instructions to employees to hold or keep any documents relevant to a specified set of issues, in order that documents such as e-mails are not deleted before they can be gathered. Once the documents have been identified, they must be preserved by photocopying or imaging them. They also need to be marked for identification and privilege, and organized in a careful and considered manner. With respect to electronic documents, one should consider securing back-up tapes for e-mails, and making copies of the computer hard drives of employees who you expect to be important witnesses in the investigation.

One should never assume that electronic documents such as e-mails are not available in an investigation. E-mails can be recovered, even if deleted. In fact, in situations where I have been informed that the hard drives had been "fried" or lost, I have found forensic specialists to recover e-mails that can be used as evidence.

In the investigations I have conducted, I have generally spent a considerable amount of time, sometimes weeks, reviewing and analyzing the documents collected prior to taking any witness interviews. Having that time to really understand the documentary evidence proved very useful when the interviews began. For each interview, I collected the relevant documents that would be used to facilitate the interview process and have those documents available for the interview.

13.8 STRATEGIES FOR CONDUCTING INTERVIEWS

It is also critical prior to conducting interviews to consider the appropriate strategy or tactic for the particular interview. As noted above, the approach used for the subject of the investigation will likely be very different from the approach used for other witnesses. Furthermore, the more that can be learned about the individual being interviewed, the better position one will be in to conduct an effective interview. Before beginning an interview, one should attempt to gather as much background information as possible concerning the prospective witness. This could include information concerning a witness's financial situation, by reviewing information on their properties, mortgages, debts or judgments levied against them, as well as their educational and employment history by reviewing transcripts and references. One should also research any prior litigation involving the critical witnesses and read transcripts of any previous depositions or trial testimony that they have undergone.

One should also speak to co-workers of the subject of the investigation to learn about the subject's tendencies and personality. One could attempt to find out whether the person would likely respond better to a more direct, or potentially intimidating, approach or whether the more conversational, easygoing approach should be utilized. In some cases, one could change the approach in the middle of an interview if the approach used is not working well. For important witnesses, it is often helpful for a second person to sit in on the interview and, if necessary, have that person take over the questions if one thinks it will facilitate a better interview.

When interviewing employees of a company in an internal investigation, it is important to establish that the interview is covered by the company's attorney-client privilege, and that the investigator represents the company, not the employee. It is also essential to point out that the privilege belongs to the company, and the company may waive the attorney-client privilege if it wishes at any time. The investigator should also specifically tell employees at the outset of the interview that the company may decide to share the details of the investigative findings at any time even without notifying the employee. One should get the employee to state on the record that they have heard and understand these instructions.

The investigator should be prepared to answer the question from an employee about whether they need their own lawyer. Prior to the interviews, the investigator should discuss with the company's General Counsel's office what approach should be taken if this question is raised. In general, investigators can answer the question by discussing whether they think the particular employee's testimony is likely to conflict with the company's positions. The investigator should know whether the company would be willing to pay for an employee's individual counsel. The investigator should make clear in the answer to the employee that he or she represents the company and, therefore, cannot really advise the employee about retaining their own counsel. If, during an investigation, there are one or two employees who may have interests adverse to the company and they ask to have their own counsel, it may be worthwhile, depending upon the facts of the matter, to provide them with and pay for their counsel. One should consider selecting counsel for them who regularly works with the company's counsel. If numerous employees are asking for their own counsel and their testimony will not likely be in conflict with the position of the company, it may make sense to tell employees that they are entitled to their own counsel, but that the firm will not pay for this representation.

There also may be instances where one needs to speak to employees who have left the company in order to conduct a thorough investigation. Company employees are generally required as a condition of their employment to speak to an investigator subject to Fifth Amendment rights. Individuals who are no longer employees of a company would not necessarily be required to speak to an investigator. However, it is important to try to reach out to persons in those situations in order to gain as many perspectives as possible about the allegations made. In my SEC investigations, I very often had to contact former employees to obtain valuable information about the facts and circumstances at issue. In the Madoff investigation, nearly all the SEC officials who had contact with Bernie Madoff had left the Agency but I was able to convince them to speak to me. One needs to persuade these individuals to speak to the investigator even when they are not compelled to do so.

One technique that can be used is to convince the former employee that information will be contained within the investigative findings about that former employee and it will be important for that former employee to have his or her side of the story incorporated into the conclusions of the report. In these cases, one may have to agree to certain conditions established by the former employee in order to obtain their agreement to conduct an interview. In the interview of Bernie Madoff that I conducted, I had to agree not to tape or record the interview. My colleague took copious notes of the interview and the information was very useful for the investigation.

Whether one uses an informal or formal approach in the interview setting, it is important that the content of the interview be documented in some way. This method may be accomplished by summarizing the interview in an informal approach and getting the interviewee to sign the summary or a statement. In a formal approach, one can either tape record the interview or have a court reporter transcribe it. While in some cases, investigators are leery of having a court reporter sitting in on the interview or even having a tape recorder on the table during the interview for fear that it will intimidate the witness, in my experience, witnesses very quickly forgot about recording devices and the interview is unaffected by them. Where witness interviews are not fully documented, there is a danger that their stories will change when those same witnesses are re-interviewed in other forums such as by the government or opposing counsel.

When conducting interviews, it is also very important to make sure that the answers one is obtaining are clear and lack ambiguity. It has happened that one thinks an answer given was clear, only to read the transcript or listen to the recording after the interview and realize that the answer given was not exactly as it was recollected to be. During important witness interviews, particularly of the subject or target of the investigation, I often think about the exact wording of the answers given and how they will read in a subsequent report. If the answer given is significant, such as an important admission, and one is not entirely convinced that the answer given was unambiguous, it is a good idea to have the witness restate the answer clearly if possible to ensure that one can document the answer later for use in the investigative report.

13.9   BRIEFING MANAGEMENT DURING AN INVESTIGATION

During the investigation, an outside investigator may be asked to brief the company's General Counsel's office regarding the progress of the investigation. However, one should be careful not to give too much information about the details of the investigation, such as information concerning the specific testimony of witnesses or the contents of important documents which have been unearthed. It is important for the investigator to retain credibility and not allow company management to influence either how the investigation is being conducted or the findings of the investigation. If briefings during the course of the investigation are given, they should be limited to procedural not substantive matters.

Similarly, during the investigation, it is critical that the company not be performing its own inquiry about the allegations simultaneous with the outside investigator conducting his or her work. When I first began conducting the Bernie Madoff investigation at the SEC, there was a request made by one of the divisions at the SEC that they be able to speak to prospective witnesses at the same time that I was conducting my investigation so that they could understand how to fix the problems within the Agency immediately. I objected to that request and made clear that I could not conduct an independent investigation while the witnesses I would be interviewing would be speaking with others about the same issues. The request was eventually denied, and I was able to have unfettered access to the witnesses and evidence without any interference.

13.10   DRAFTING THE INVESTIGATIVE REPORT

The investigative report is a very significant part of the investigation. While there are occasions where companies wish to have an oral, rather than written briefing of the findings, in most instances, the findings are documented in an investigative report. In those cases, it is important that the investigative report be well-written, well-sourced, and persuasive in nature. The report is not a legal brief, and should not be written in a one-sided manner in an argument-style format. The testimony should be described without editorial content, and the documents quoted verbatim as often as possible. Where there is evidence that is in dispute or on both sides of an issue, this should be set forth clearly. There should be source documents cited or footnoted in the report for every point that is made. I tend to prefer writing long reports with numerous footnotes and appendices so that the report contains all the information necessary to substantiate the conclusions or findings made.

The report of the investigation I conducted on the Bernie Madoff $50 billion Ponzi scheme while I was at the SEC was 457 pages long and contained over 500 footnotes. For very long reports, it is generally helpful to include an executive summary at the beginning of the report so that the reader can understand the report's conclusions without having to read the entire report.

13.11   INCORPORATING RECOMMENDATIONS FOR IMPROVEMENT

Where an internal investigation finds wrongdoing, the report should include specific and concrete recommendations to take disciplinary action against the wrongdoers, and also to improve the structures or controls within the company that allowed the wrongdoing to occur. If significant recommendations are going to be made about a company's operations, it is helpful for the investigator to meet with company representatives before finalizing the recommendations portion of the investigation to ensure that the recommendations given are ones that may be implemented within a reasonable time frame after the investigation is concluded.

After the investigation, it is important that the company be prepared to implement the recommendations and demonstrate, if necessary, to a regulatory body how they have learned from the investigation and remedied the deficiencies in their operations, and can attest to the fact that the wrongdoing will not reoccur in the future. Where recommendations have been implemented, it may be advisable for companies to test the improved structures or controls a couple of years later to ensure that they are operating effectively. Generally, companies should conduct reviews of their compliance programs after any significant allegations have been brought forward to ensure that the procedures in place are working appropriately.

13.12 PROTECTING FILES ASSOCIATED WITH INTERNAL INVESTIGATION

As the materials used in conducting an internal investigation are often sought in litigation arising out of the same incident that led to the investigation, it may be advantageous for a firm to take the proper steps to protect those materials from being produced. In a June 2014 D.C. Circuit Appellate decision, the D.C. Appeals Court overturned a lower court's ruling that ordered a company to produce internal investigation files in response to a discovery request made by a former employee who was suing the company.[2] The Court found that the files could be protected by the attorney-client privilege as long as obtaining or providing legal advice was one of the significant purposes of the internal investigation.

---

[2]See *In re Kellogg Brown & Root, Inc., et al.*, No. 14-5055 (D.C. Cir. June 27, 2014).

Accordingly, under the D.C. Circuit's analysis and the analysis in other jurisdictions,[3] a company may have more than one significant reason for conducting an internal investigation, including regulatory requirements or a corporate compliance policy, without waiving the attorney-client privilege. However, it is important to document that at least one of the significant reasons for conducting the investigation was to obtain legal advice by making clear that the investigation was conducted "at the direction of" or "under the auspices of" the legal department. Employees being interviewed can also be specifically advised at the beginning of the interview that one of the purposes of the interview was to help the company obtain legal advice. In addition, one should label clearly those documents that are intended to be covered by the attorney-client privilege or the work product doctrine. One should be careful, however, to label documents judiciously as excessive marking of documents may weaken the privilege for the sensitive documents that really need the protection.

The report should also be addressed to the General Counsel's office, which should document its review of the report and any advice offered to the company as a result of the investigation's findings. If possible, the threat of litigation should also be documented.

The D.C. Circuit Court also stressed that the attorney-client privilege only protects against the disclosure of confidential or privileged *communications*. The confidentiality of communications can be maintained by restricting dissemination within the company, and maintaining investigative files and documentation apart from general corporate files.

---

[3]The seminal case on this matter is the U.S. Supreme Court decision in *Upjohn Co. v. United States*, 449 U.S. 383 (1981), in which Upjohn's General Counsel, outside counsel, and the Chairman of the Board decided to conduct an internal investigation of an allegation made by independent accountants conducting an audit that certain payments had been made to foreign government officials. After the investigation was concluded, the company voluntarily submitted a preliminary report to the SEC and the Internal Revenue Service ("IRS"), and the IRS sought all files relative to the investigation. Upjohn objected to the production of these materials on attorney-client privilege and work product grounds. In a unanimous 9-0 decision, the Supreme Court held for Upjohn and determined that the communications were protected by attorney-client privilege when protection was necessary to defend against litigation.

13.13   RETAINING THE INVESTIGATIVE REPORT

Where an internal investigation finds no wrongdoing, the investigative report should be kept as evidence that the allegations were taken seriously and that the matter was investigated thoroughly and the allegations were found to lack merit. A written report can also be important if there is a subsequent claim of misconduct or retaliation.

Conducting thorough and comprehensive investigations is extremely important in convincing regulatory authorities that any misconduct or wrongdoing that may have occurred was limited to a "rogue" employee or office, and that appropriate action has been taken against the wrongdoers. In the FCPA context, companies have significantly lowered their eventual penalties by conducting investigations and performing remedial work. Internal investigations can also provide companies with important knowledge about their potential exposure so they can make intelligent business decisions and can anticipate the direction in which the government investigators may be heading. In these circumstances, knowledge is power and this knowledge can only be obtained if the company allows an independent, thorough, and credible investigation to be conducted.

CHAPTER 14

Conclusion

Having served as the Inspector General of the SEC from 2007 to 2012, I issued many of the reports that triggered Congressional criticism of the SEC and federal regulators in general in the aftermath of the financial crisis, including an audit report that detailed the SEC's failures in oversight of Bear Stearns, as well as investigative reports that were critical of the SEC for failing to uncover the Bernie Madoff and Allen Stanford Ponzi schemes. My reports described how the SEC was in a position to halt the deterioration of Bear Stearns and expose Madoff and Stanford's frauds, but failed to conduct competent regulatory oversight. I watched first-hand how Congressional officials excoriated the SEC and its management and heard the whispers about the possibility that the SEC should be abolished.

Yet, in the end, the SEC was not abolished, broken up, or merged with another entity, nor has its structure been impacted in any significant way. In fact, I also watched Congress react to the SEC and regulatory failings by enacting the Dodd-Frank Act, which gave the SEC significant new responsibilities and duties. I recall testifying before Congress on more than one occasion and fielding a question posed by a Senator or Congressman that was predicated upon the assumption that the SEC's failures were related to a lack of resources. It was clear in many Congressional officials' view that if the SEC had just been given more resources, they would have caught Madoff and Stanford and stopped Bear Stearns from going under. I did not necessarily agree with this assumption and, on more than one occasion, tried to explain that at least in connection with the Madoff and Stanford cases, it was a lack of competence rather than a lack of resources that led to the SEC's failures. While my office made numerous substantive recommendations to fix the underlying problems at the SEC which the SEC agreed to and implemented, fewer of these types of changes came from Congress. Instead, the Dodd-Frank Act imposed many new requirements on the SEC, and many new instruments and products in the marketplace became subject to regulatory oversight. While most would acknowledge that these new requirements provided more protection to investors, it is less clear that entities such as the SEC engaged in the oversight have been significantly strengthened and improved.

Accordingly, financial investors cannot necessarily rely exclusively on the SEC and other regulatory Agencies to police potential frauds or illegal conduct. Companies and individual investors must conduct their own due diligence to ensure that they are not being defrauded and cannot assume that just because an entity is regulated by the SEC or other Agency, they have been properly examined for a potential Ponzi scheme or other fraud.

14.1 OVERLAPPING JURISDICTIONS AFTER THE DODD-FRANK ACT

In addition, because of the decision to place new responsibilities upon the SEC and other regulatory Agencies with the enactment of the Dodd-Frank Act, companies are facing even greater uncertainty and pressures associated with overlapping and inconsistent regulations. In fact, post the Dodd-Frank Act, the Agencies themselves have sometimes faced the difficult question of which Agency has jurisdiction over a particular product. Some financial products simply have attributes that make it difficult to determine which Agency has jurisdiction over them. For example, financial engineers have developed products with attributes of both futures and securities, thus helping to confuse the line between futures and securities regulation. This uncertainty has caused delays in bringing new products to market, has been costly and confusing, and has impeded innovation and competition.

The overlapping has not been limited to jurisdiction over products. There has also been a convergence of marketplaces and market participants such that the same entity is subject to the regulatory authority of both the SEC and the CFTC.[1] The confusion has been so great that at one point, it was actually suggested that Congress enact legislation to let either the SEC or CFTC petition a federal appeals court to resolve a dispute over which Agency has jurisdiction over a particular product.

Moreover, even though in the aftermath of the regulatory failings, there was an effort made to harmonize the regulatory policies of the SEC and CFTC with a goal of applying consistent standards to market participants, this effort was never completed. In June 2009, the U.S. Treasury issued a white paper that outlined a roadmap for restoring confidence in the integrity of the financial system and asked the SEC and the CFTC to prepare a report that would identify differences between their regulatory schemes, would determine whether the differences were justified by differences in the nature of the markets, and otherwise would recommend changes to harmonize futures and securities regulation.[2] In response, in August 2009, the SEC and the CFTC announced that they would hold a joint meeting to hear from the public regarding the most pressing issues for regulatory harmonization.[3] The two Agencies invited experts and representatives of stakeholders to speak at the public meeting. Public comment was also invited. The event took place in September 2009 with the participation of all sitting Commissioners of both Agencies.[4]

In October, the SEC and CFTC issued a joint report identifying areas where the Agencies' regulatory schemes differ and recommending actions to address those differences. The report included 20 recommendations to enhance enforcement powers, strengthen

---

[1]In December 2014, for example, Timothy Massad, the chairman of the CFTC, stated in testimony before the U.S. Senate Committee on Agriculture, Nutrition & Forestry that the CFTC's authority may include certain types of virtual currency such as bitcoin, in addition to the SEC's acknowledged authority over this same currency. http://darkcoin.ws/united-states-cftc-claims-jurisdiction-over-bitcoin/.

[2]http://www.treasury.gov/initiatives/Documents/FinalReport_web.pdf.

[3]http://www.sec.gov/news/press/2009/2009-186.htm.

[4]http://www.sec.gov/news/press/2009/2009-218.htm.

market and intermediary oversight, and improve operational coordination. In May 2010, the SEC and CFTC announced the formation of a joint committee that would address emerging and ongoing issues between the two Agencies to follow up on the recommendations included in the Agencies' harmonization report.[5] While there were some efforts made for the two Agencies to work more cooperatively together, in my view, most onlookers would acknowledge today that a great deal more work is needed to harmonize the regulatory policies of the CFTC and SEC and the goal of applying consistent standards to market participants has not been achieved.

In addition, in today's regulatory environment, there is little discussion anymore about consolidation of the CFTC and SEC or any significant structural changes to either Agency even though former House Financial Services Committee Chairman Barney Frank stated just before he retired in 2012 that "the existence of a separate SEC and CFTC is the single largest structural defect in our regulatory system."[6] I believe that combining the two Agencies could in fact help to plug regulatory gaps and streamline rulemaking by unifying functions in one Agency. As the markets regulated by the two Agencies have converged, there is little reason for the continued fragmentation. Yet, the primary reason given for the lack of momentum after the financial crisis for the merger of the two Agencies was the fact that the SEC falls under the jurisdiction of the U.S. Senate Banking and House Financial Services committees, while the U.S. Senate and House Agriculture committees have jurisdiction over the CFTC. It was the turf battles rather than any substantive and learned decision-making process that led the consolidation efforts to fail.

Yet, the reality today is that for many financial institutions, more than one regulatory Agency has overlapping jurisdiction, and none of them has clear authority. In addition to the impacts on the companies themselves, this fragmentation makes it difficult for any Agency or individual to understand the broader markets or to coordinate appropriate interagency actions to address growing issues and problems.

---

[5] http://www.cftc.gov/PressRoom/PressReleases/pr5820-10.
[6] http://democrats.financialservices.house.gov/news/documentsingle.aspx?DocumentID=382948.

In addition, multiple and sometimes competing regulatory oversight can eventually lead to a lack of communication, the weakening of regulatory standards and principles, overlapping and inefficient jurisdictions, and an inability to see the full picture of the markets. Further, these issues can be exacerbated when the self-regulatory organizations also do not coordinate their efforts and effectively communicate with one another or with the regulatory Agencies.

14.2 REGULATORY FAILURES POST-FINANCIAL CRISIS

Yet, even since the financial crisis and the Madoff scandal, there have been more examples of significant regulatory failures. For instance, having two regulators conducting oversight, the SEC and the CFTC, did not prevent MF Global from failing in October 2011. In fact, according to a critique of MF Global's collapse released by Republican members of the U.S. House of Representatives Committee on Financial Services' oversight subcommittee, the SEC and the CFTC failed to share critical information about MF Global's collapse and could have saved some investor funds if the Agencies had worked together.

The report stated as follows:

The apparent inability of these agencies to coordinate their regulatory oversight efforts or to share vital information with one another, coupled with the reality that futures products, markets and market participants have converged, compel the subcommittee to recommend that Congress explore whether customers and investors would be better served if the SEC and the CFTC streamline their operations or merge into a single financial regulatory agency that would have oversight of capital markets as a whole.[7]

According to the report, the CFTC and the SEC worked at "cross purposes" in the weeks and months before MF Global's bankruptcy

---

[7]http://financialservices.house.gov/uploadedfiles/11-15-12_mf_global_staff_report_001.pdf.

filing, failing to communicate about key meetings with MF Global executives regarding the firm's liquidity and the $184 million capital infusion imposed by FINRA to reflect the risks of its bond portfolio. The SEC and the CFTC also issued conflicting guidance for the $220 million that MF Global had set aside to protect broker-dealer customers according to the report. The report concluded that "had the SEC and the CFTC coordinated their supervision of [MF Global] and had they shared critical information about MF Global, they might have gained a more complete understanding of the company's deteriorating financial health, and they might have taken action to better protect the company's customers and investors before it collapsed."[8]

14.3 IMPROVING OF COORDINATION BETWEEN REGULATORY AGENCIES

One successful effort to improve coordination among regulatory Agencies was the establishment of the Financial Stability Oversight Council ("FSOC") pursuant to the Dodd-Frank Act. The FSOC is charged with three primary purposes: (1) to identify risks to the financial stability of the United States that could arise from the material financial distress or failure, or ongoing activities, of large, interconnected bank holding companies or nonbank financial companies, or that could arise outside the financial services marketplace; (2) to promote market discipline, by eliminating expectations on the part of shareholders, creditors, and counterparties of such companies that the U.S. government will shield them from losses in the event of failure; and (3) to respond to emerging threats to the stability of the U.S. financial system.[9] The FSOC consists of 10 voting members and five nonvoting members and brings together the expertise of federal financial regulators, state regulators, and an insurance expert, and includes representatives of the Treasury Department, the Federal Reserve, the OCC, the Bureau of Consumer Financial Protection, the

---

[8]Ibid.

[9]Financial Stability Oversight Council, 2011 Annual Report, http://www.treasury.gov/initiatives/fsoc/Documents/FSOCAR2011.pdf.

SEC, the FDIC, the CFTC, the Federal Housing Finance Agency, and the NCUA.[10]

The most significant activity by FSOC to date has been its work in connection with designating nonbank financial entities as systemically important financial institutions ("SIFIs") which has the effect of subjecting the designated institution to additional regulatory oversight and requiring it to hold more capital. Proponents of this effort state that regulating systemically important firms reduces the risk that failure of such a firm could destabilize the financial system and harm the real economy. However, these designations as well as the process underlying the designations have been met with significant controversy and lawsuits.

While serving as Inspector General of the SEC, I participated in the Council of Inspectors General on Financial Oversight ("CIGFO") which was also established by the Dodd-Frank Act to facilitate sharing of information among the Inspectors General of the Agencies and departments in the FSOC. The CIGFO was also tasked with joint oversight of the FSOC to ensure that effective coordination and cooperation take place among the departments and regulatory Agencies. From my perspective on CIGFO, I was able to see that the activities of the FSOC showed some promise in that apart from the specific activities of the FSOC such as the SIFI designations, the fact that the FSOC had been created did force these regulators to meet and make a greater effort at coordination on some of the larger market-related financial issues. Prior to the FSOC, I did not see much coordination at all between the SEC and CFTC, for example, and even if one disagrees with particular decisions made by the FSOC, the mere fact they are coordinating their efforts and talking to one another is a positive trend in my opinion. However, while the FSOC is analyzing these broader financial market issues in a more cohesive manner, the day-to-day requirements of the regulatory Agencies have not been impacted significantly. The regulatory overlap and confusion remains even though it is a detriment both to the financial firms and to the investors that need to be protected.

---

[10]http://www.treasury.gov/initiatives/fsoc/Documents/FSOC%202014%20Annual%20Report.pdf.

14.4 UNDERSTANDING THE REGULATORY CLIMATE

As a result, companies need to understand that the regulatory climate is unlikely to change in the near future and accordingly, companies must have the necessary tools to combat the overlapping regulatory requirements. As this book illustrates, the most effective way to address the regulatory pressures from the many entities that regulate, examine, and investigate companies is to address each one separately and try to understand their particular motivations and agendas. Defending an SEC Enforcement action involves very different strategies than defending a CFTC, FINRA, or NFA Enforcement action. The availability of resources to the Agency conducting the investigation as well as the level of expertise and their respective philosophies with respect to settlement must be understood in order to put forward the best approach to defending the matter. Similarly, the information sought in an examination as well as the sophistication of the examiner will vary greatly depending upon whether the examination is conducted by the SEC, FINRA, or the NFA. As a result, the approach taken by the firm being examined must be different as well.

An FCPA investigation that is commenced by either the SEC or the DOJ, or by both simultaneously, must be defended with a proper understanding of the motivations of the particular prosecutors or Enforcement attorneys. Further, companies need to be particularly careful about how they interact with internal whistleblowers and must understand that the way in which they conduct internal investigations will significantly impact the level of their exposure. Perhaps most importantly, in order to respond appropriately to regulatory requirements, companies must develop effective and well-thought-out policies and procedures, ensure accountability within the organization, and establish an ethical culture throughout the organization.

Finally, companies should appreciate the fact that there are ways in which they can impact the regulatory process such as participating in rulemakings, whether as part of a trade association or by simply providing feedback themselves that is unique to their company. In addition, establishing collegial and positive relationships with regulators can be almost as important as having good relationships with one's customers. This can be accomplished by understanding each individual regulator's mission, perspective, and processes; listening to the regulators' concerns; being organized, open, and responsive in regulatory communications; keeping promises made to regulators; and showing the regulators that your goal is to comply with the regulations and to cooperate with the regulators. Adopting this advice and with the assistance of qualified professionals with particular expertise and understanding of the regulations and regulators, companies can face these regulatory challenges and take the necessary steps to satisfy the regulators while still allowing their businesses to grow and flourish.

About the Website

Please visit this book's companion website at www.wiley.com/go/kotzregulation for more information and further reading in regulatory compliance.

The password to download the models is: secreg15

Index

Compiled by INDEXING SPECIALISTS (UK) Ltd.